Vancouver's Endearing Splendour of Flowers Collection

Rowena Kong

Annie Ho

Ronnie Kong

Rowena Kong
2022

First Printing: 2022

ISBN: 978-1-990782-06-0

Introduction

Located on the western end of the lower mainland of British Columbia in Canada, Vancouver is a city blessed with one of the mildest weather conditions in the country befitting for a variety of blossoms through the seasons of the year. From late winter's Primrose to autumn's Aster, there is a wide range of flower genus to choose from for one's gardening pleasure. This guide serves as a convenient alphabetical listing of both the more popular and lesser known flower varieties which one can find available in garden centres as well as featured in public parks within nature-loving Vancouver.

1. African Daisy (Osteospermum)
   Colour: White; Purple; Pink; Yellow
   First Bloom: April
   Scent: None
   Petal Size: Medium

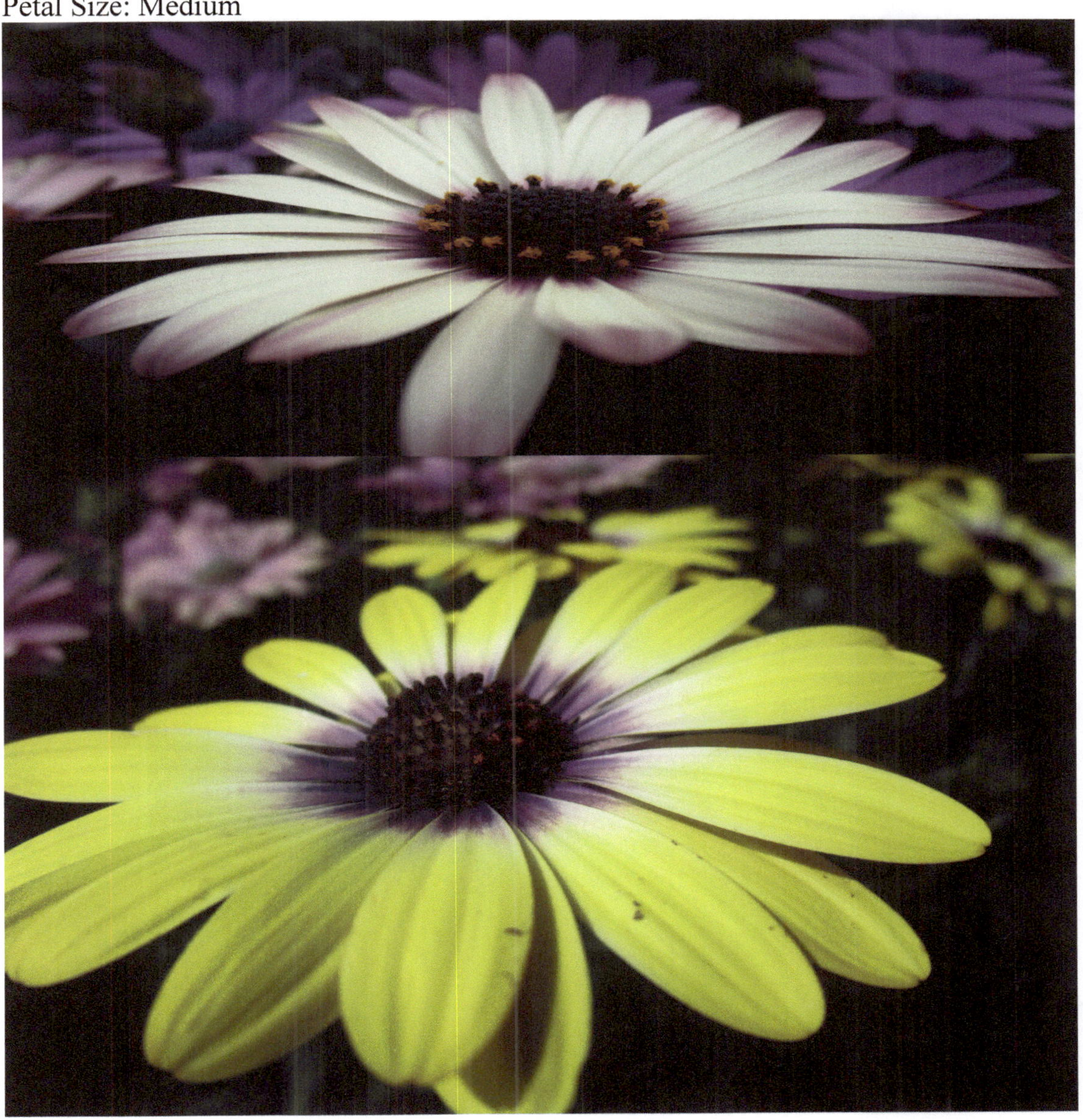

2. Allium "Onion Flower"
   Colour: Purple; Violet
   First Bloom: April
   Scent: None
   Petal Size: Tiny

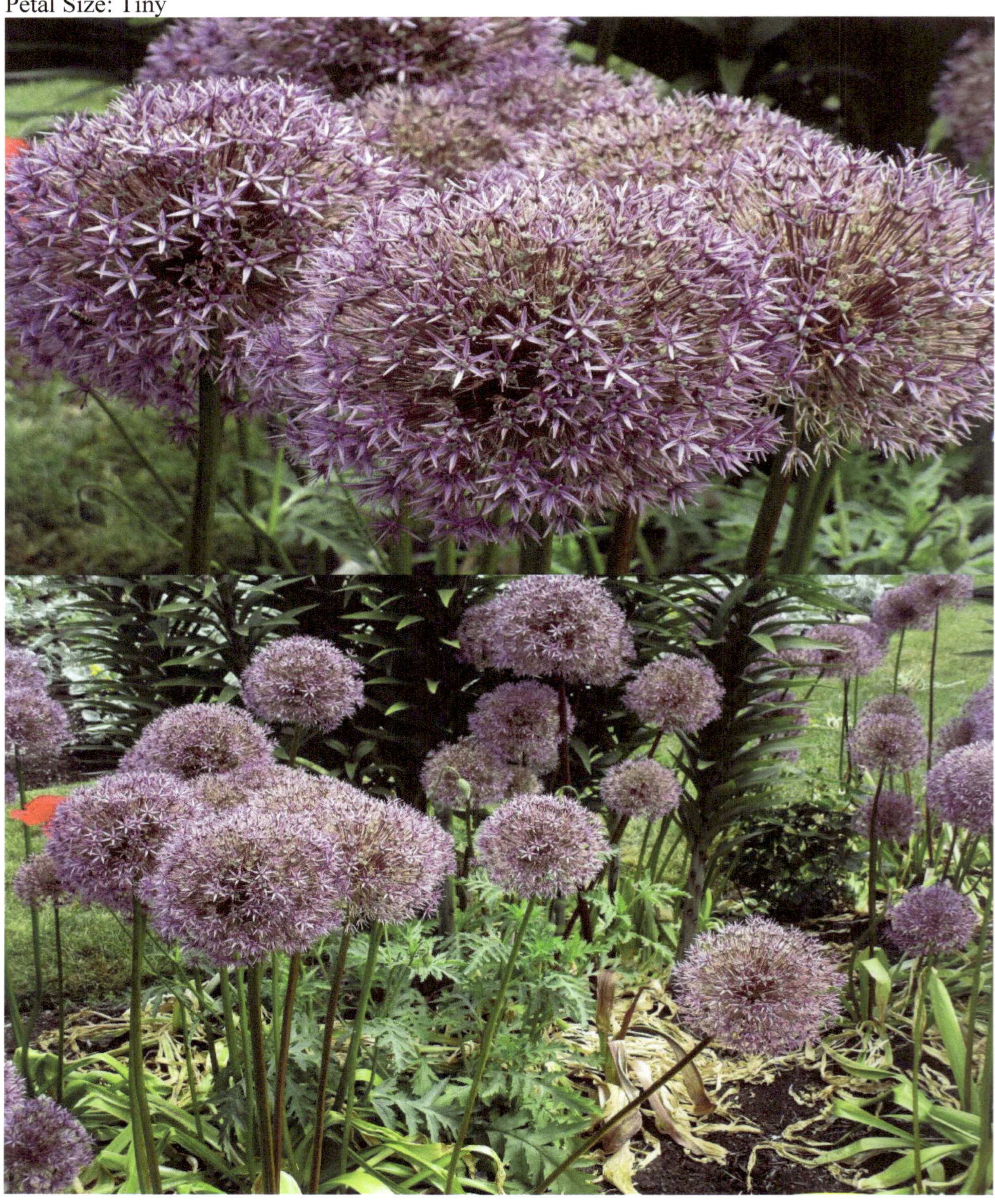

3. Alyssum (Lobularia maritima)
    Colour: White; Purple; Green
    First Bloom: April
    Scent: Strong
    Petal Size: Small

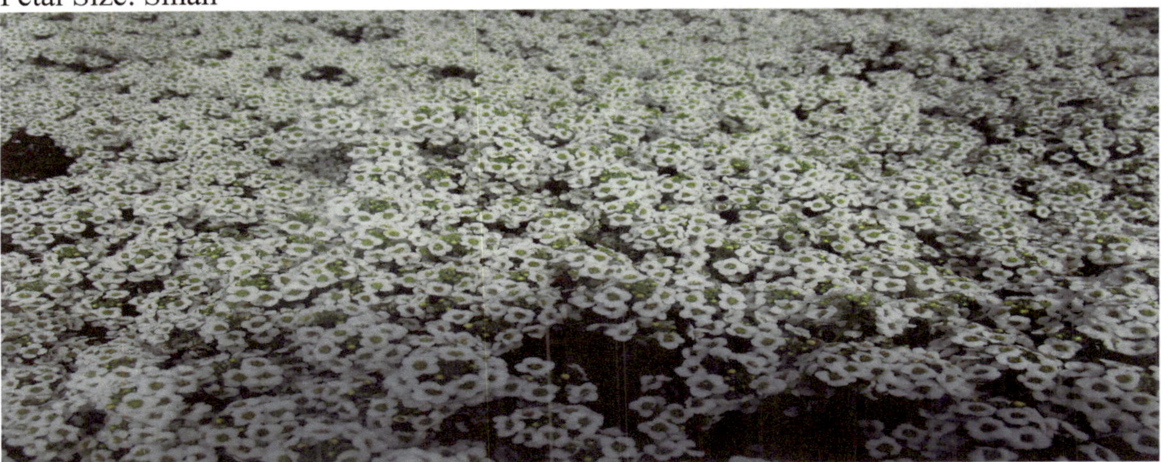

4. Aster (Aster)
    Colour: Purple; Orange
    First Bloom: September
    Scent: Mild
    Petal Size: Medium

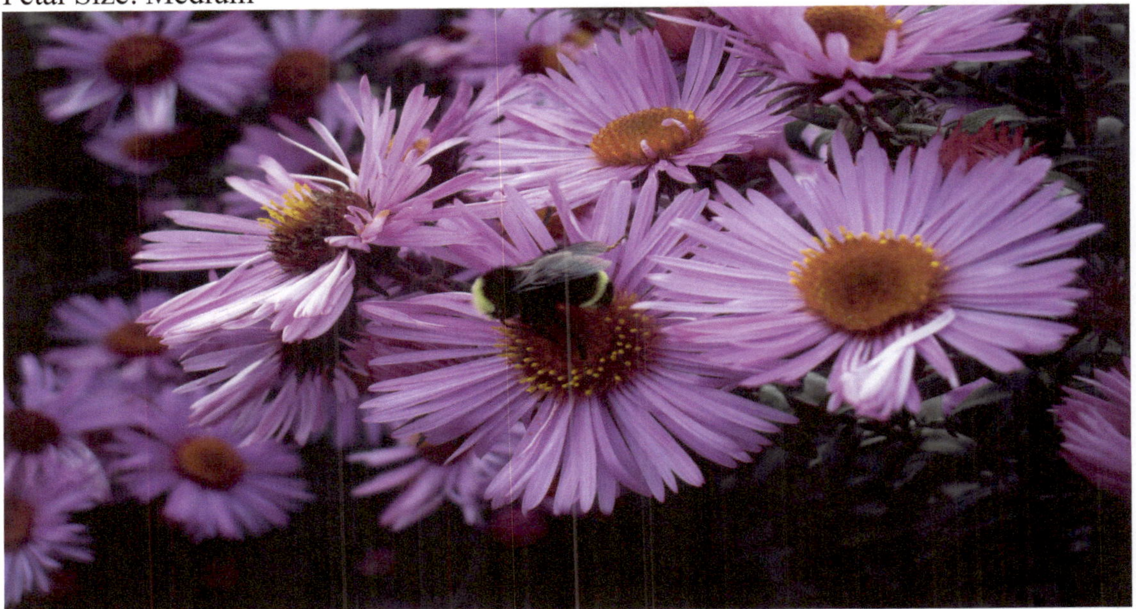

Aster is particularly attractive to bees in autumn during its full bloom, when these helpers of pollination get to work with brimming enthusiasm.

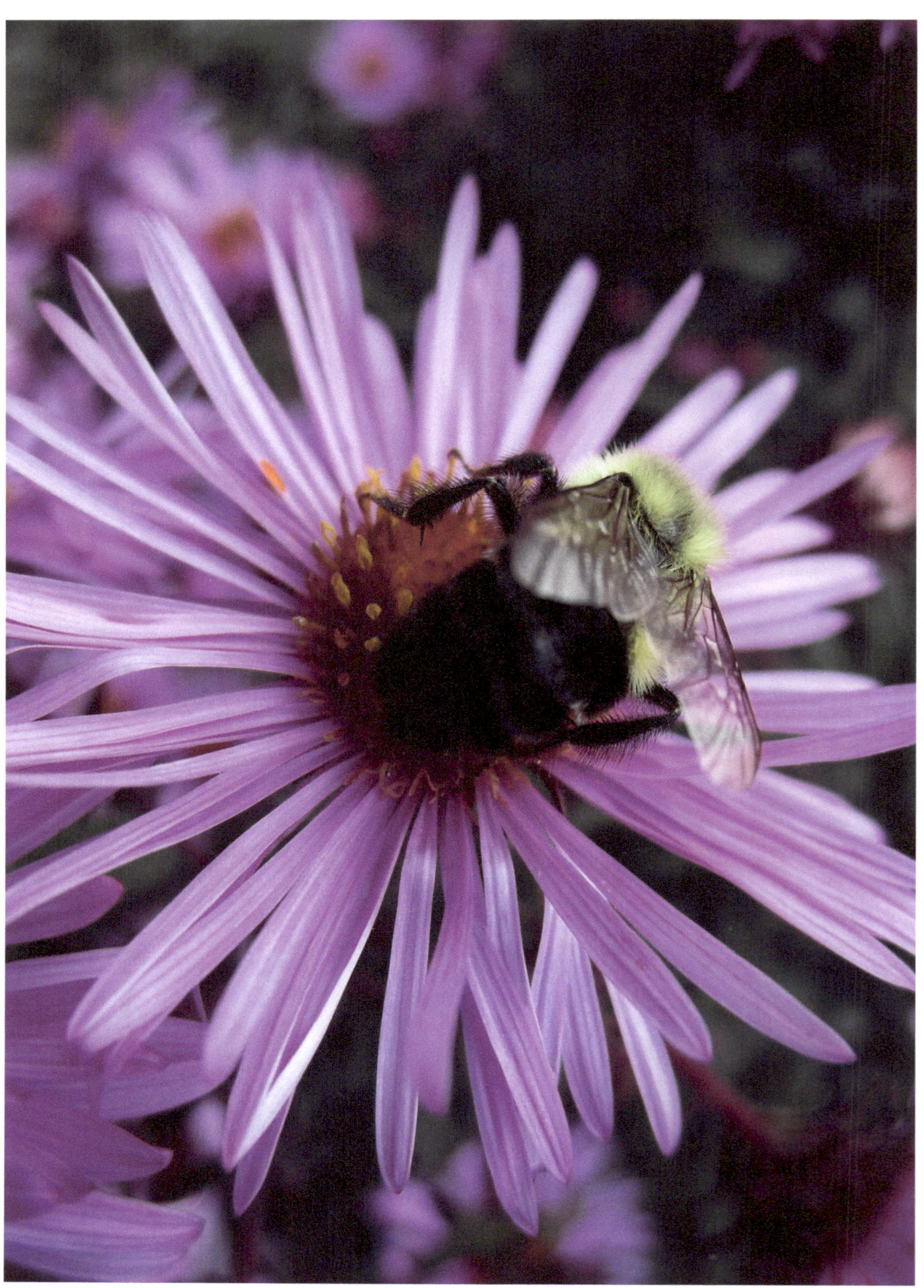

5. Bacopa (Bacopa monnieri)
   Colour: White; Yellow
   First Bloom: April
   Amount of Sun Needed: Moderate to Full
   Scent: None
   Petal Size: Considerably Small

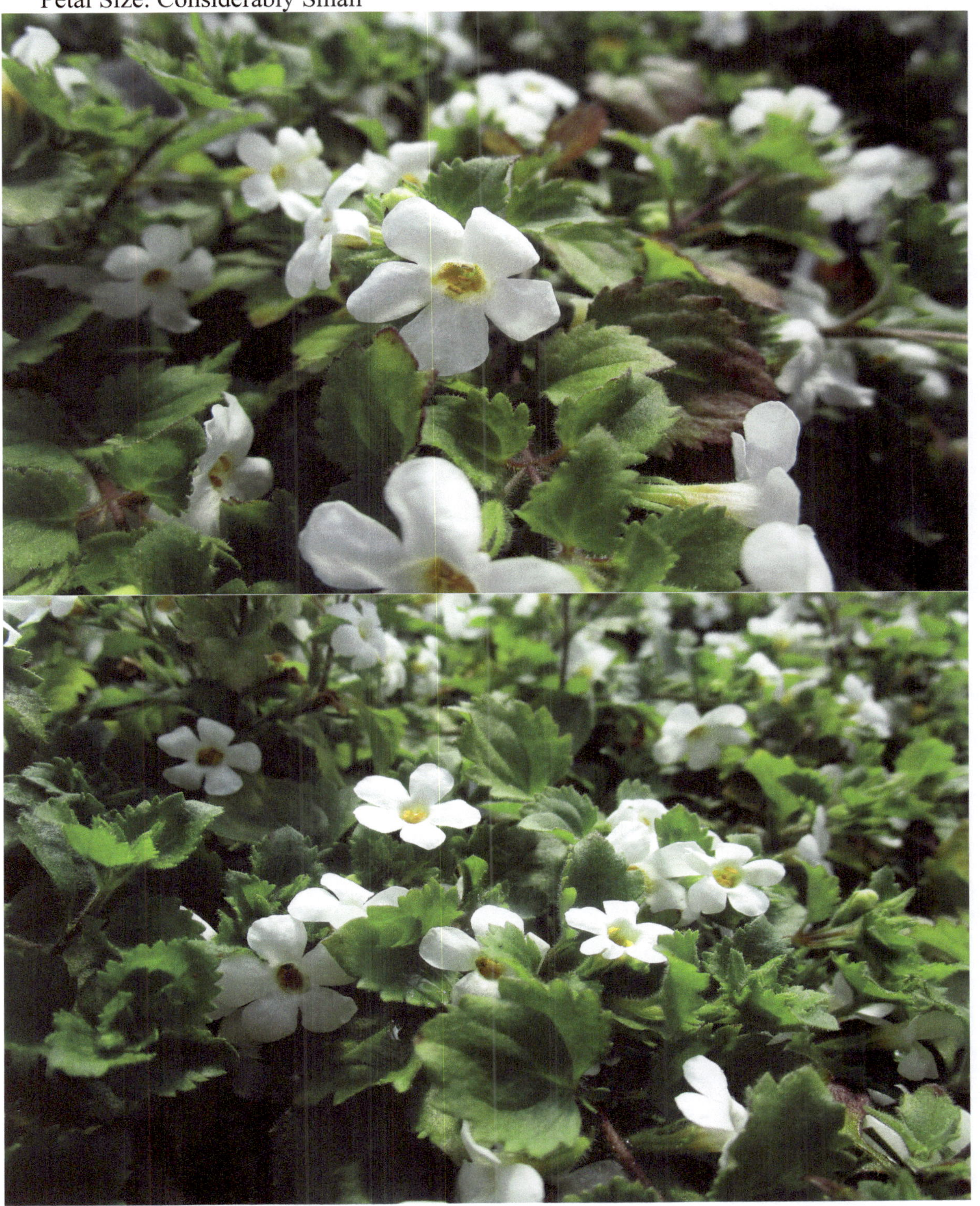

6. Bonica Rose (Rosa 'Bonica 82')
    Colour: Pink; White
    First Bloom: June
    Amount of Sun Needed: Moderate to Full
    Scent: None
    Petal Size: Medium

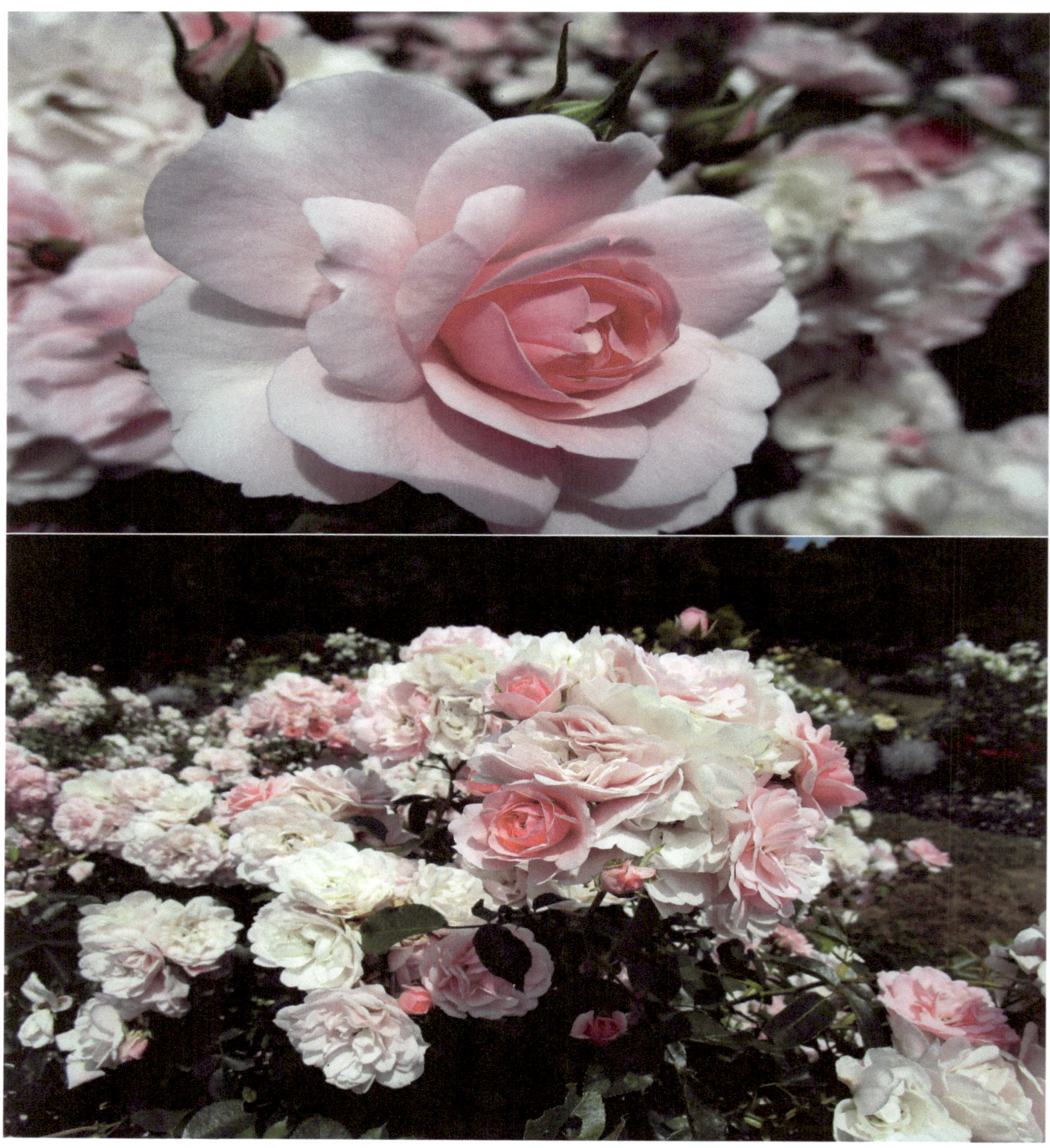

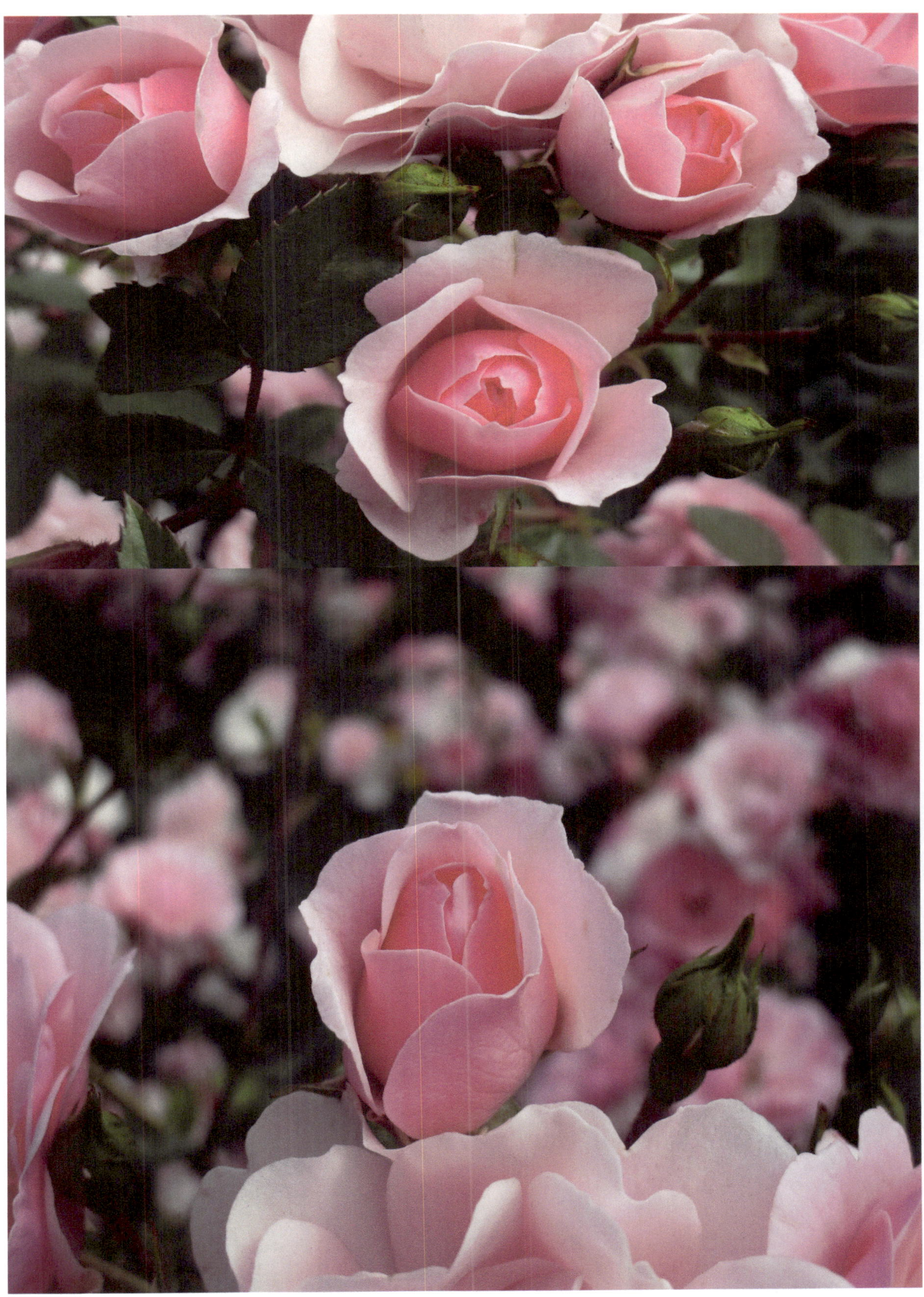

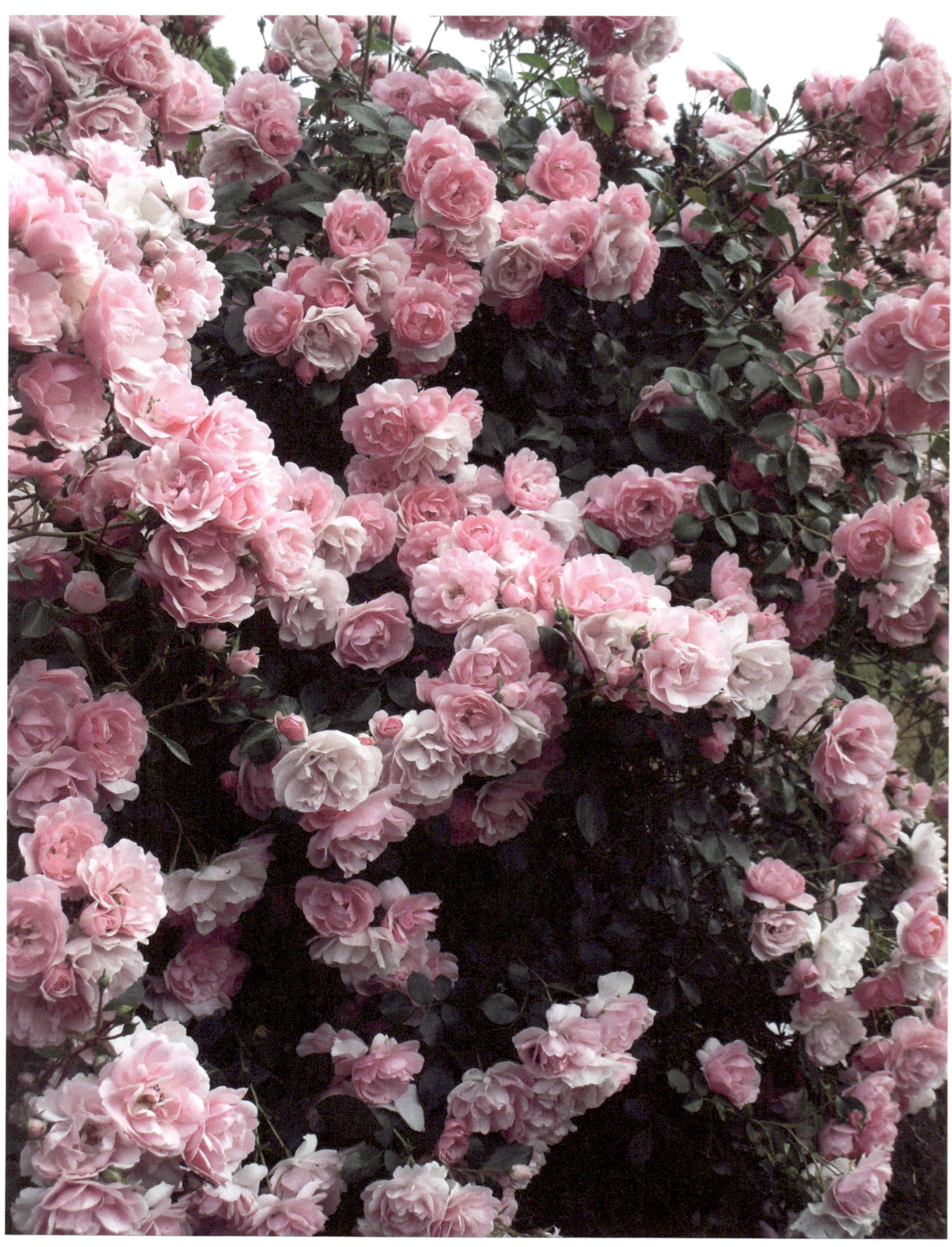

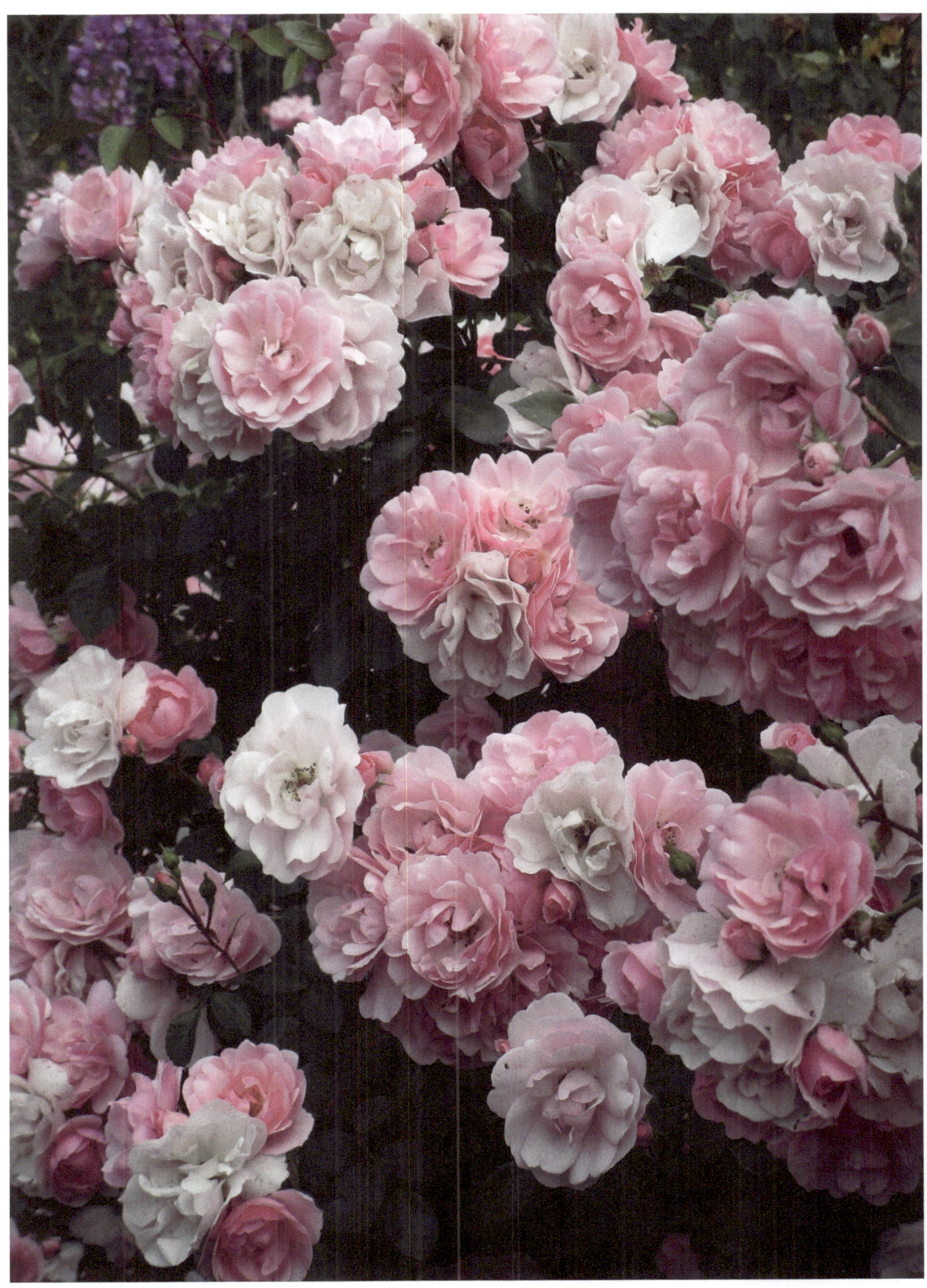

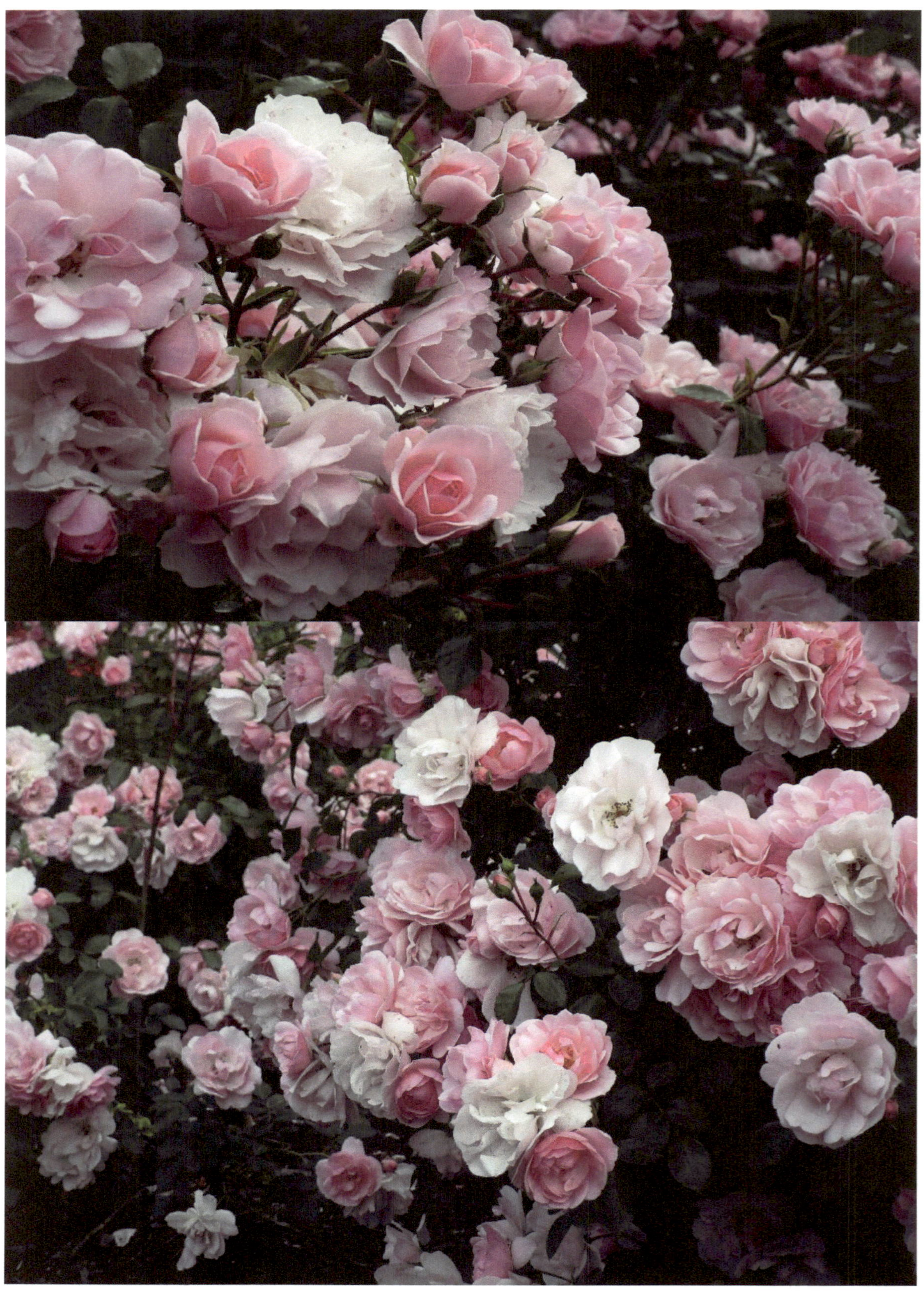

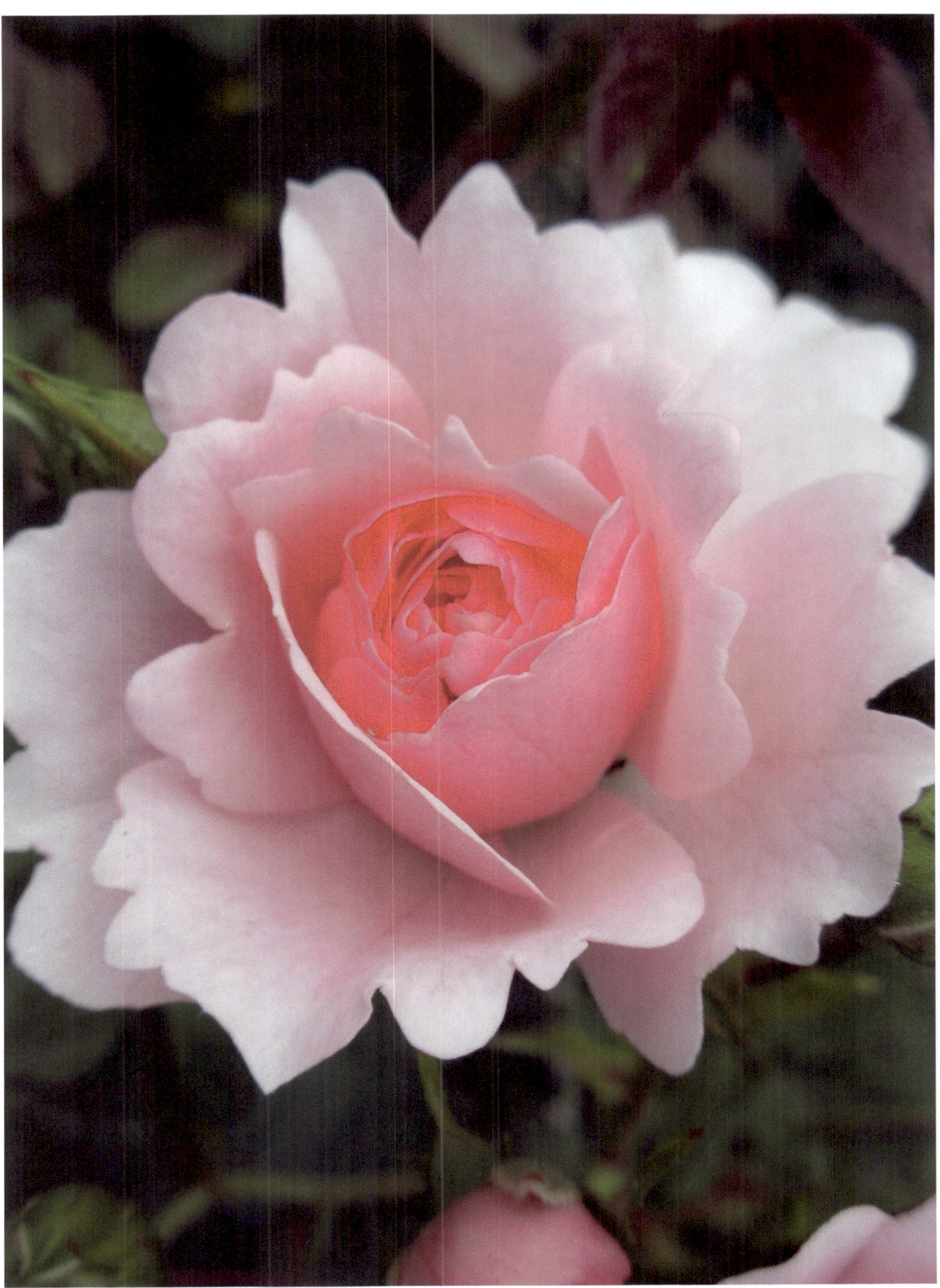

7. Candytuft (Iberis)
    Colour: Purple; Violet: White; Pink; Yellow; Varied
    First Bloom: July
    Amount of Sun Needed: Mild to Moderate
    Scent: None
    Petal Size: Small

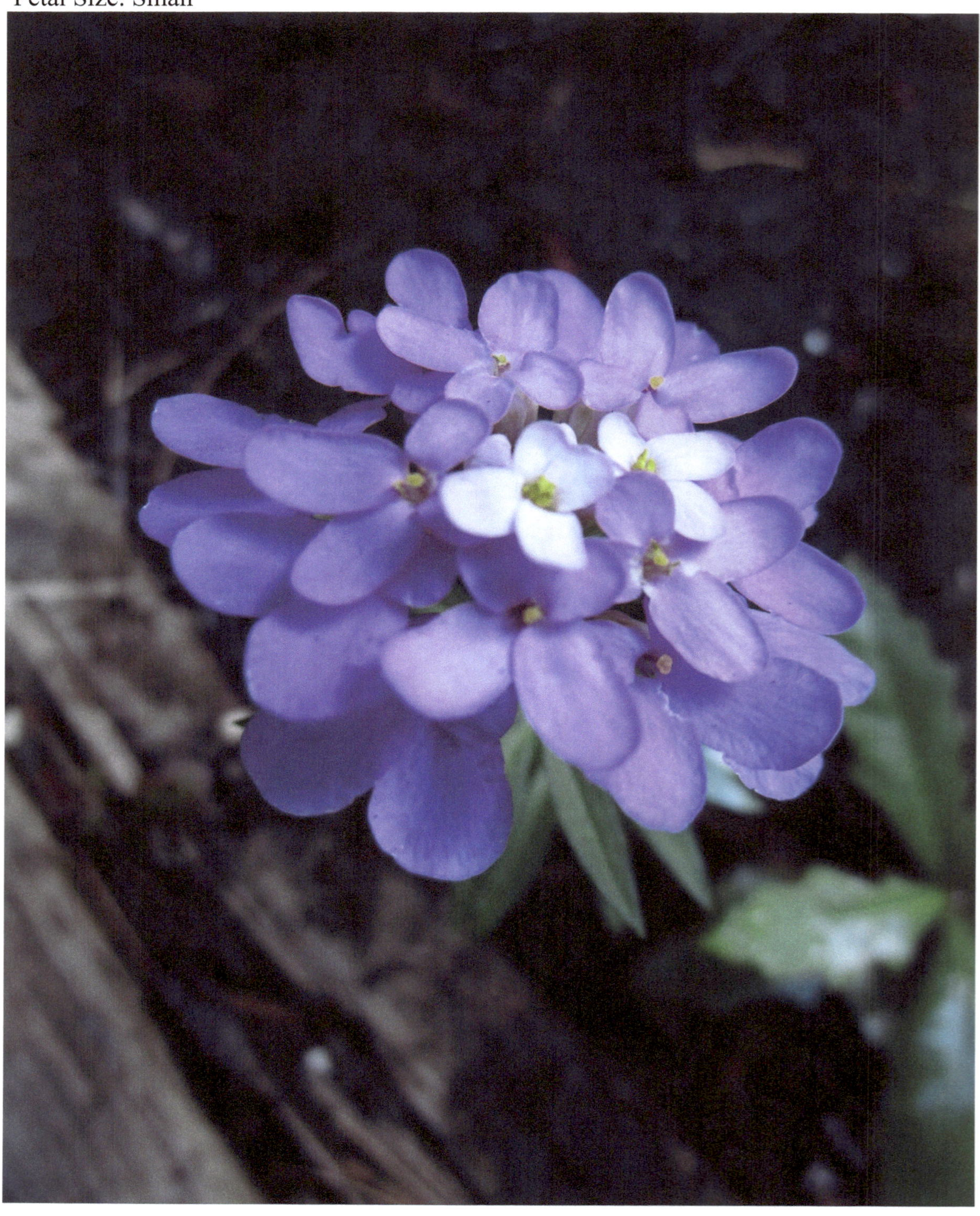

8. "Caramel Fairytale" Rose by Floribunda(Rosa)
    Colour: Caramel-like; Yellowish Orange
    First Bloom: June
    Amount of Sun Needed: Moderate to Full
    Scent: None
    Petal Size: Medium

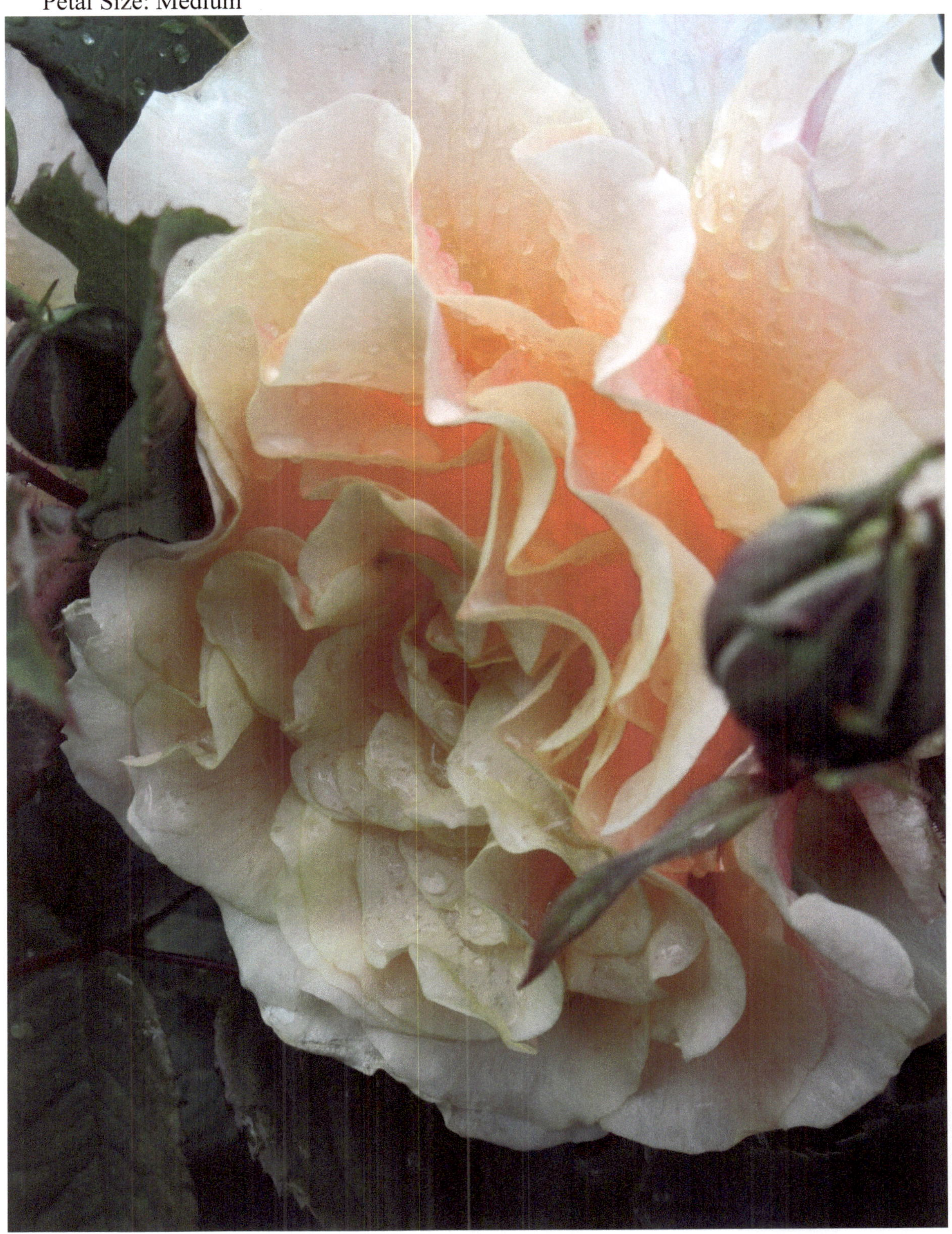

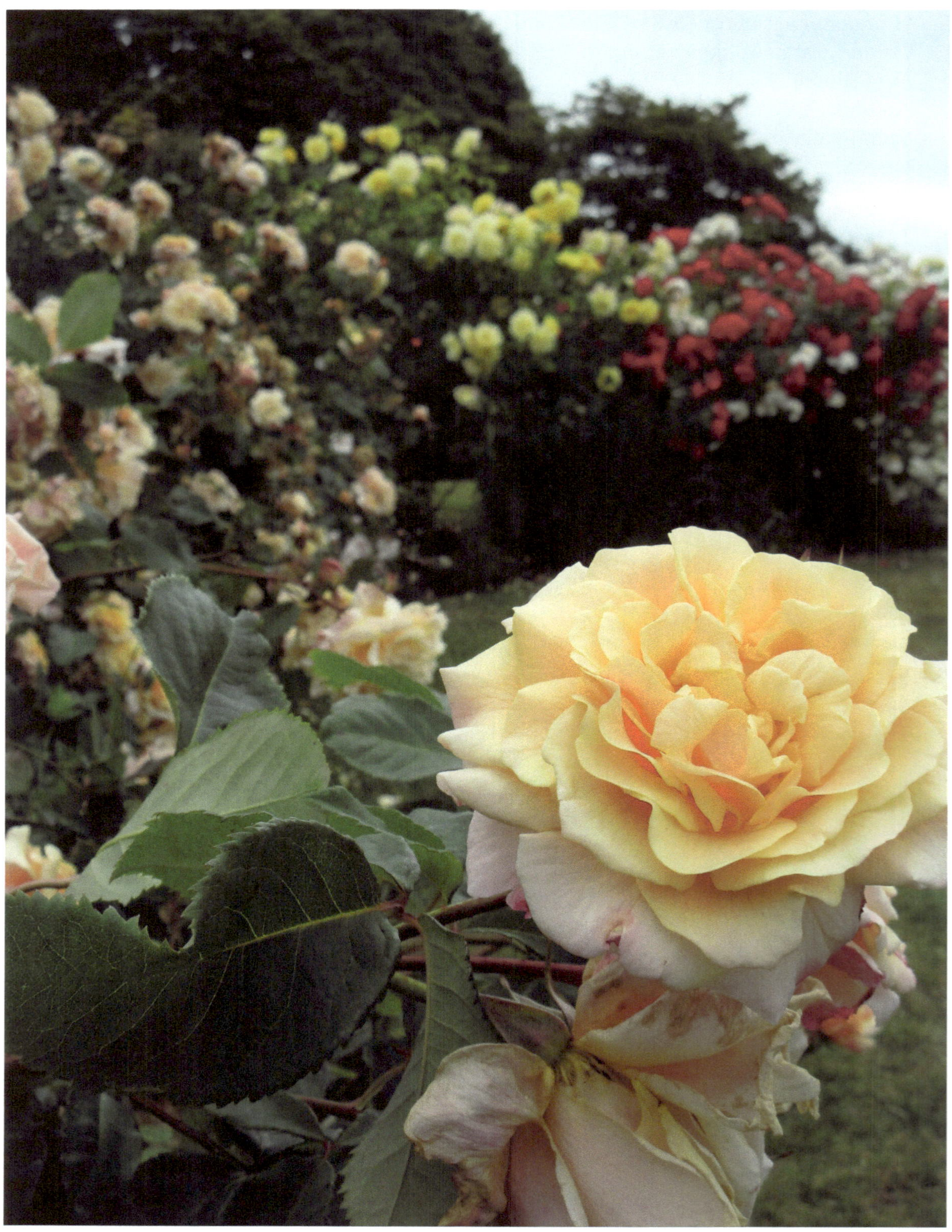

9. Carnation (Dianthus caryophyllus)
   Colour: Pink; Red; White
   First Bloom: March
   Amount of Sun Needed: Full
   Scent: None
   Petal Size: Small to Fairly Medium

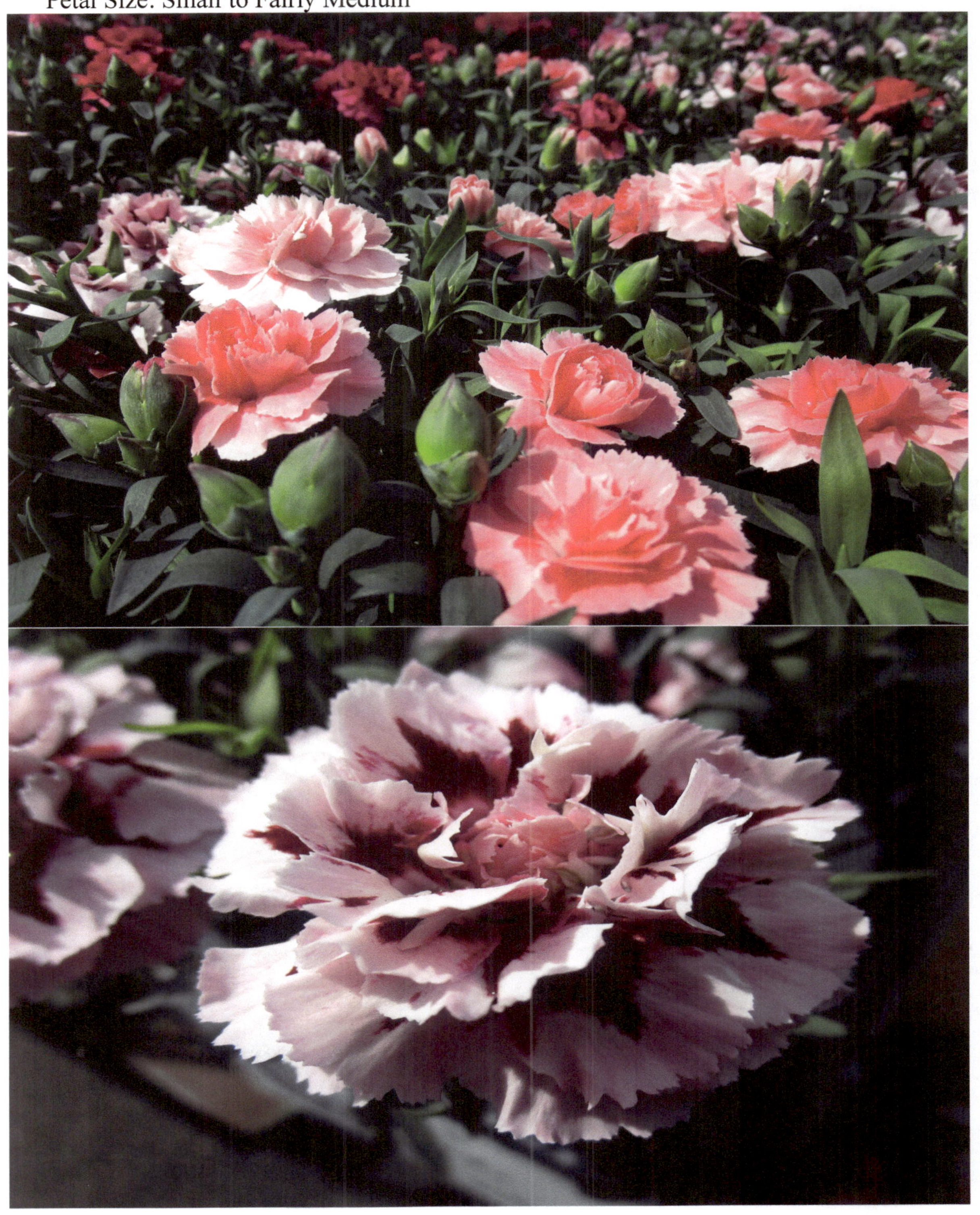

10. Cherry Blossom (Prunus serrulata)
   Colour: Pink; White
   First Bloom: Mid-March
   Amount of Sun Needed: Moderate
   Scent: Mild
   Petal Size: Small to Large

"Akebono"

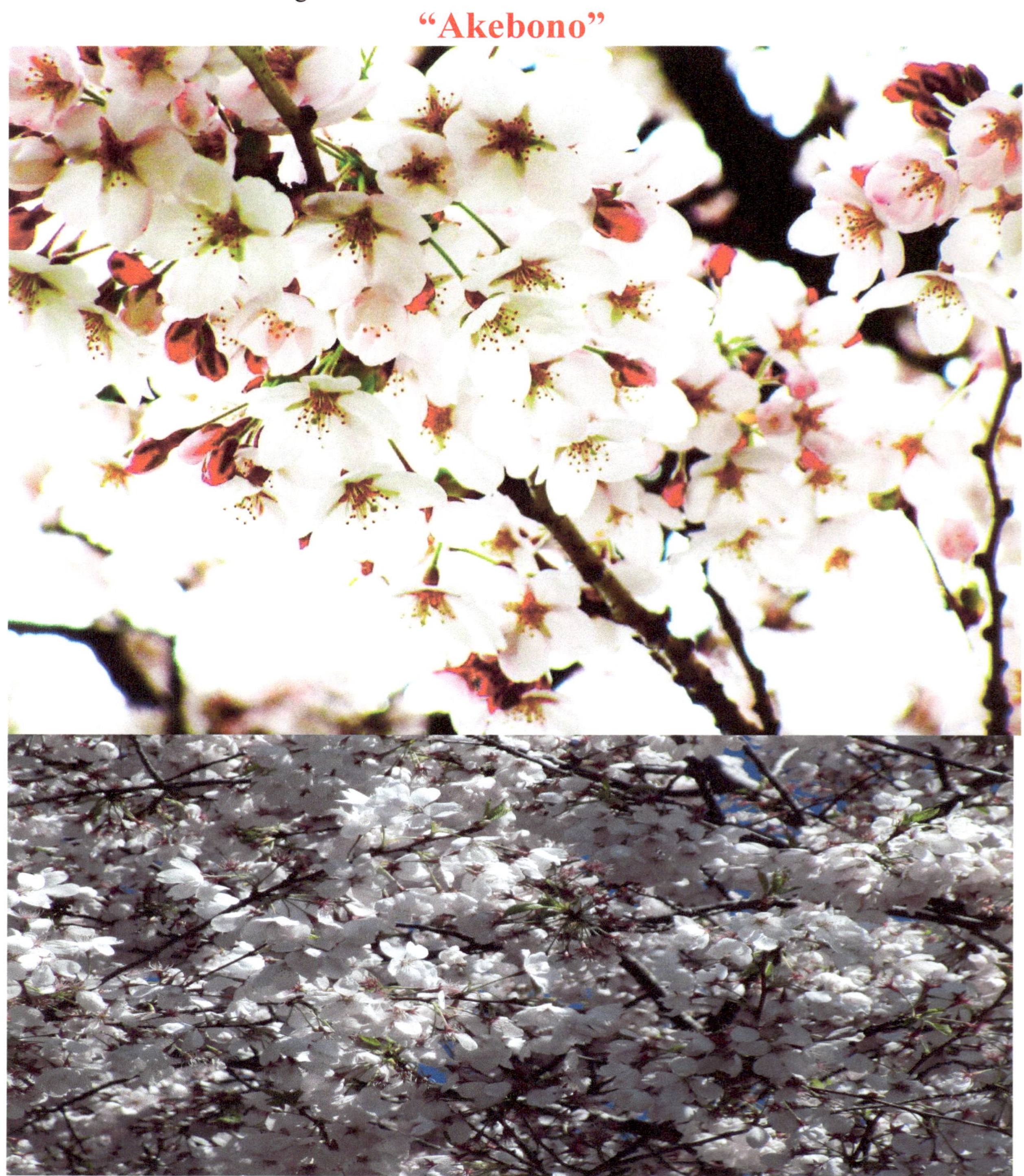

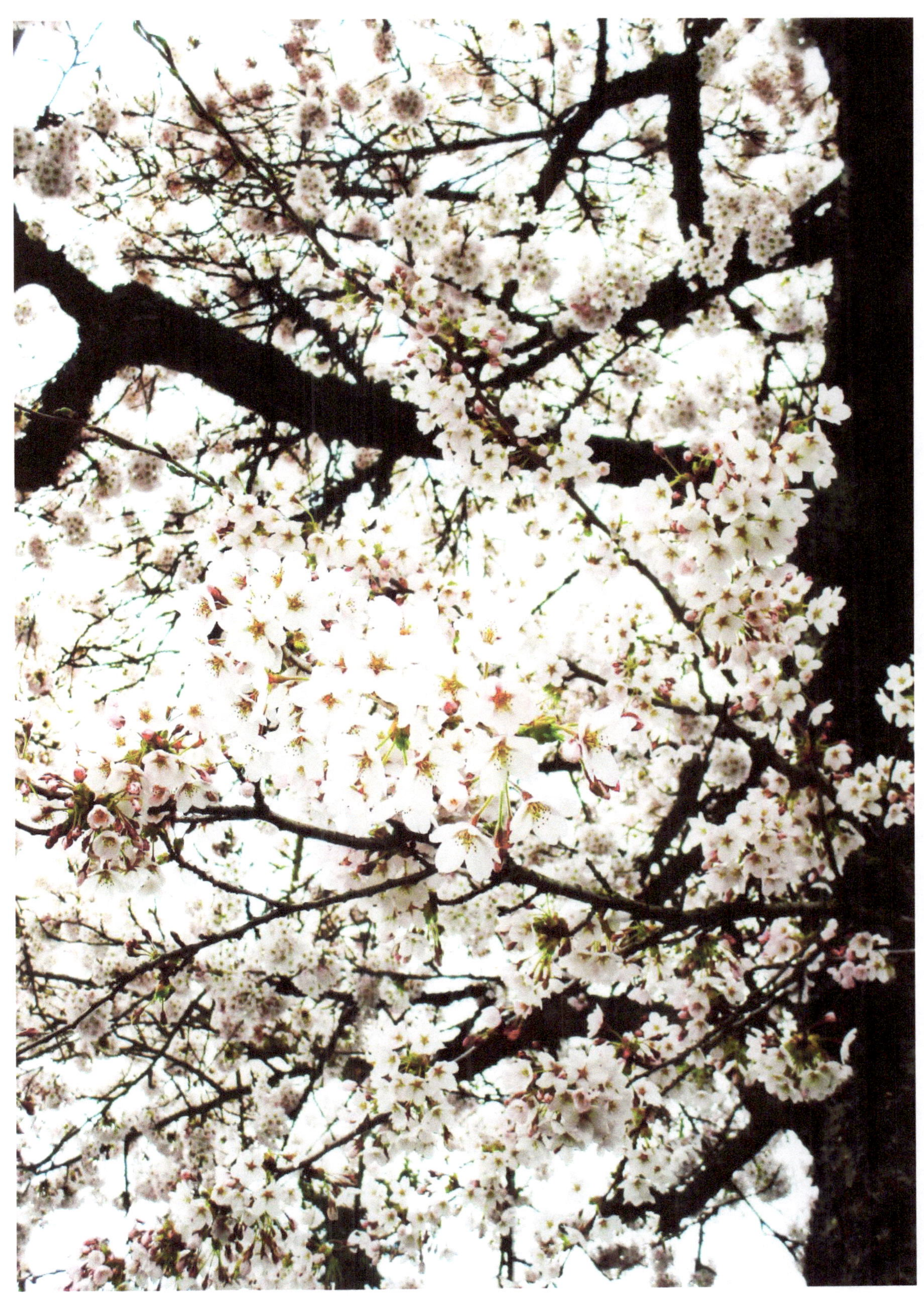

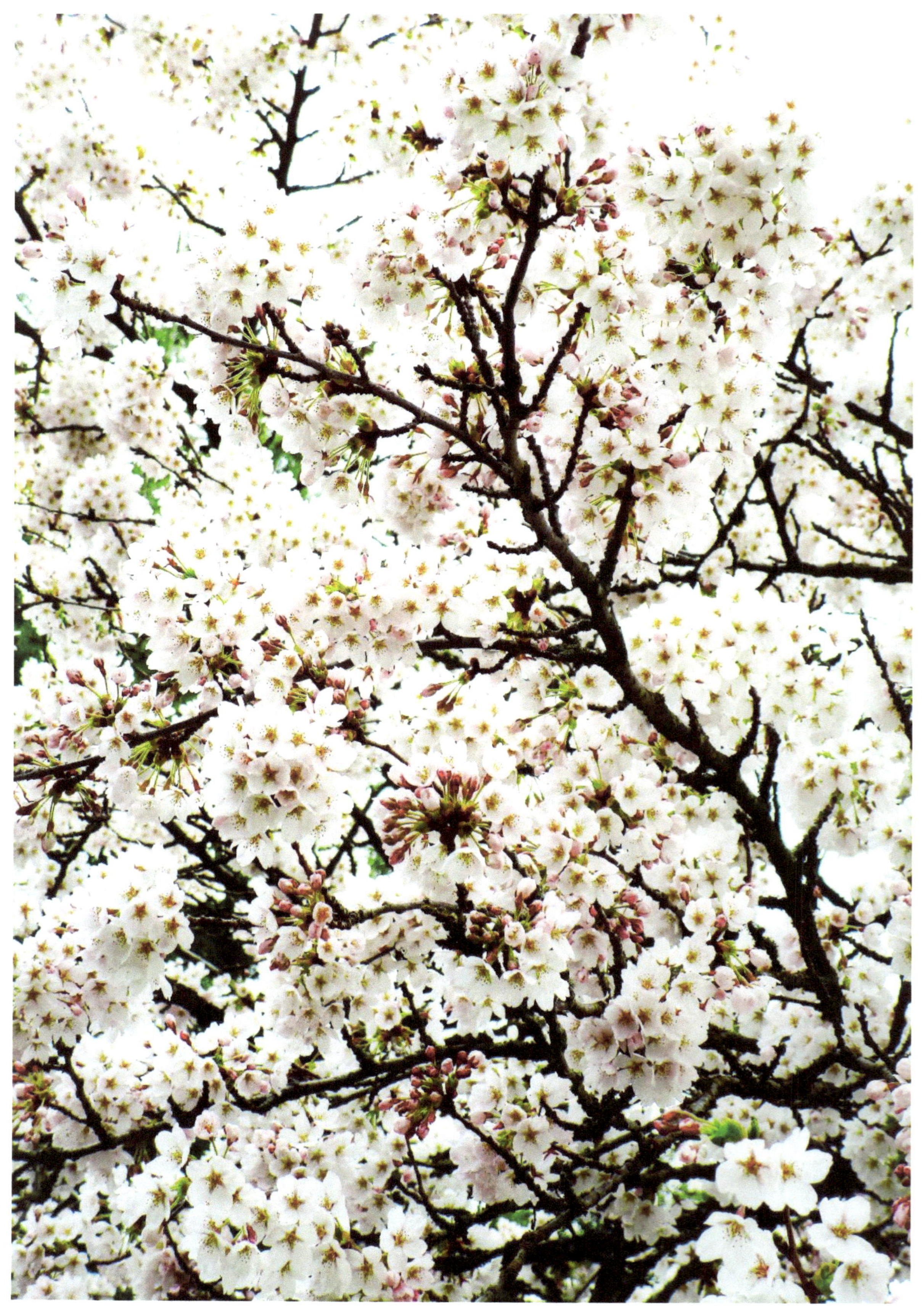

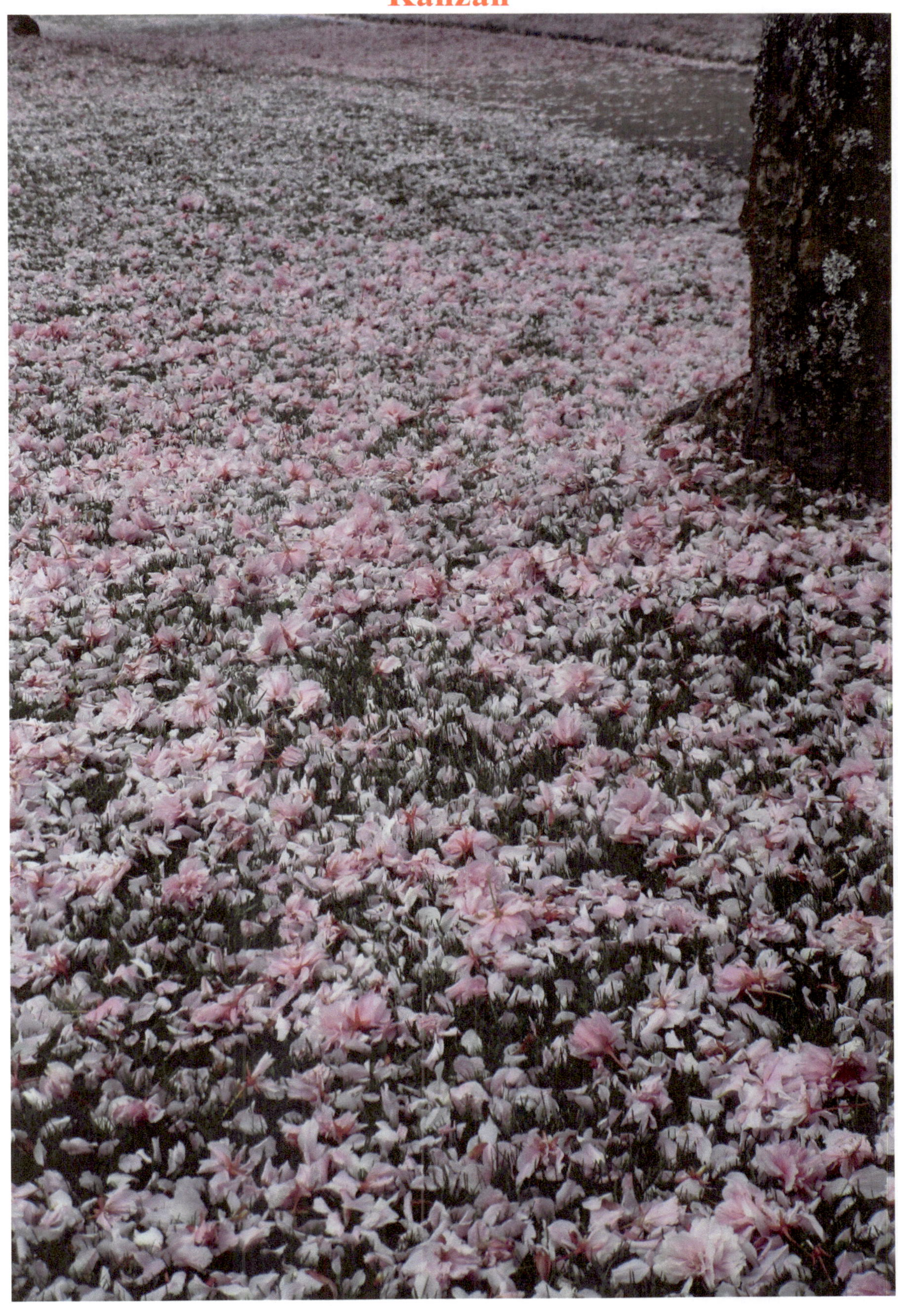

"Kanzan"

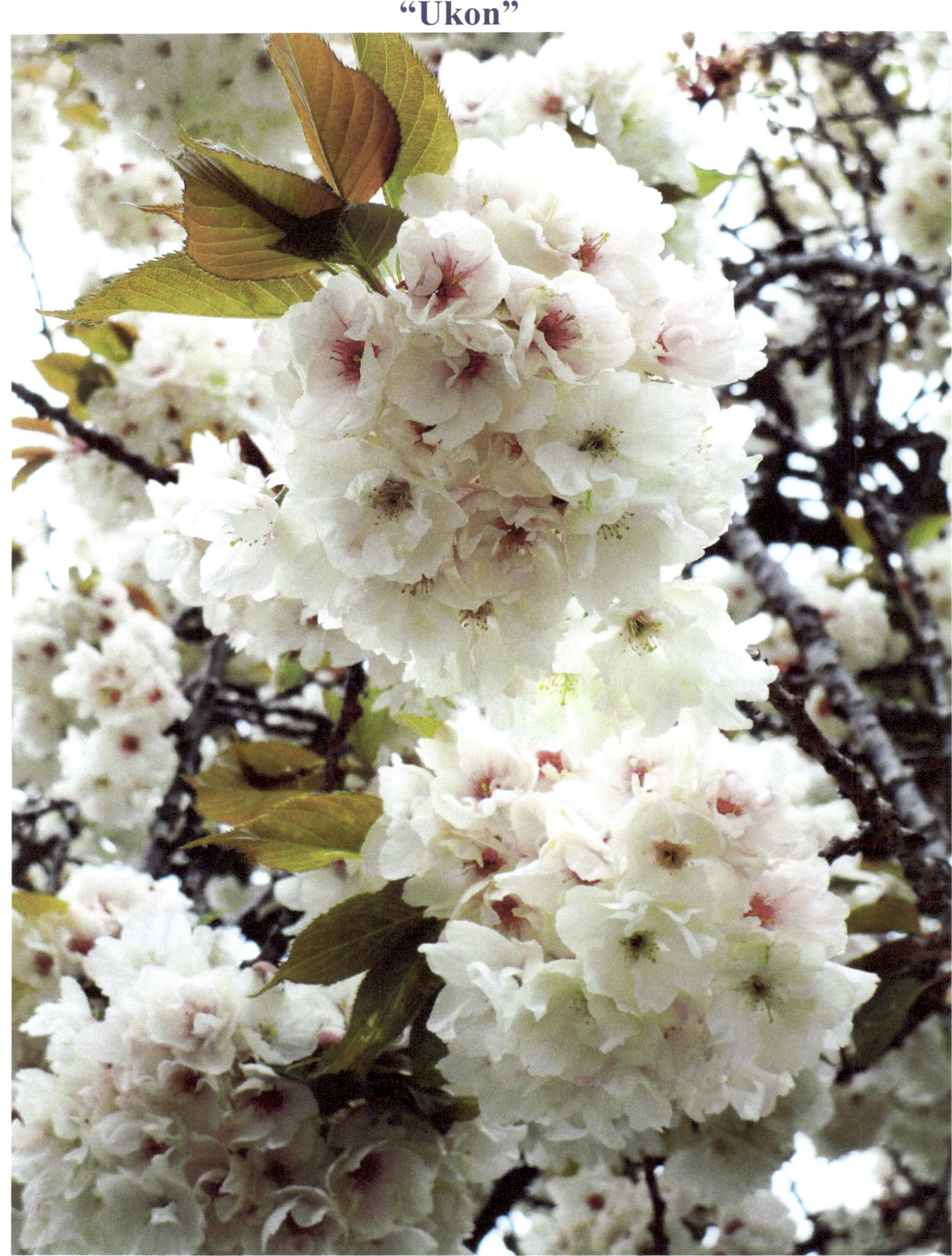

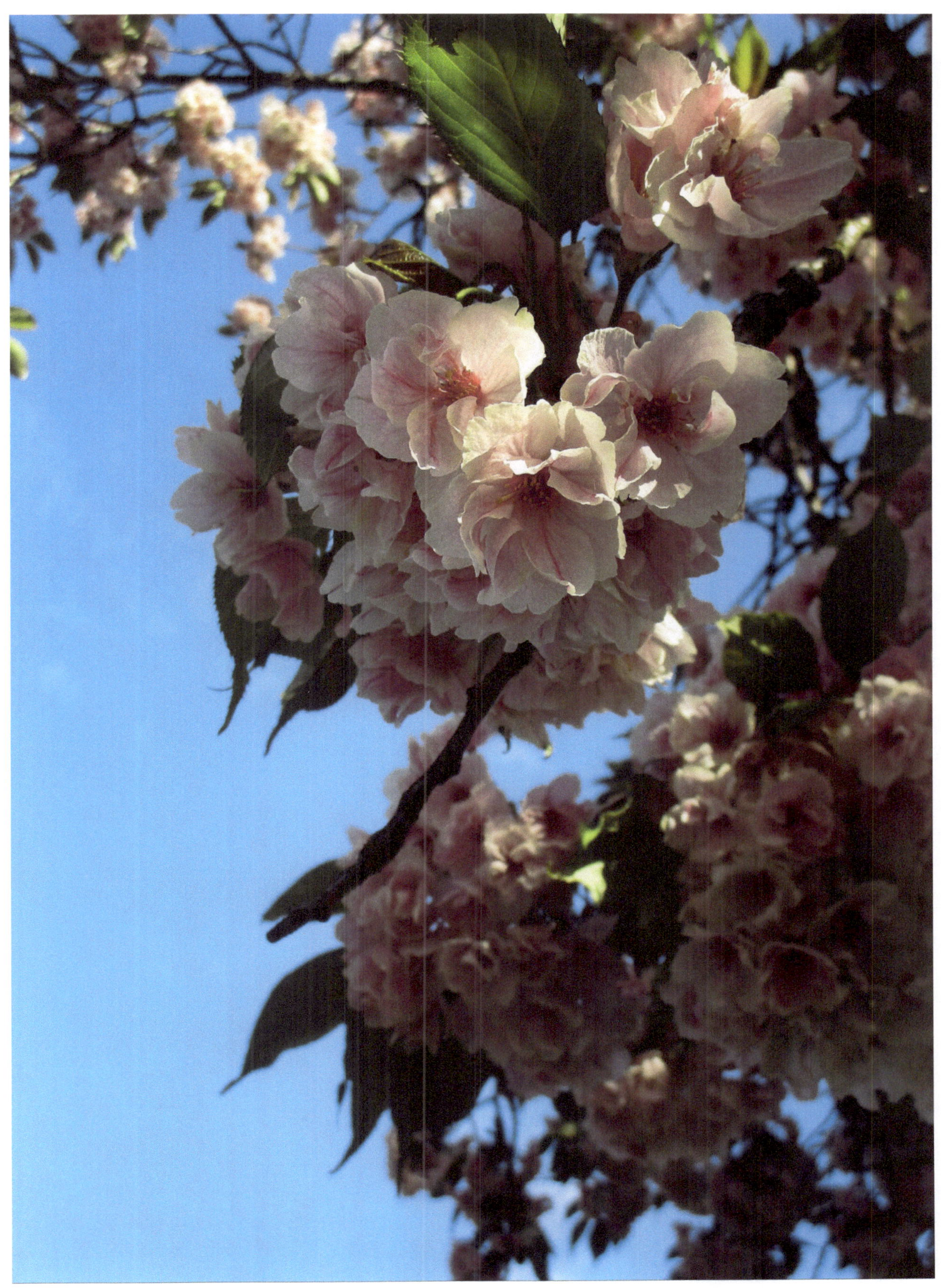

11. Cosmos (Cosmos bipinnatus)
    Colour: Pink; Light Purple; Red; White; Yellow
    First Bloom: May
    Scent: None
    Petal Size: Medium

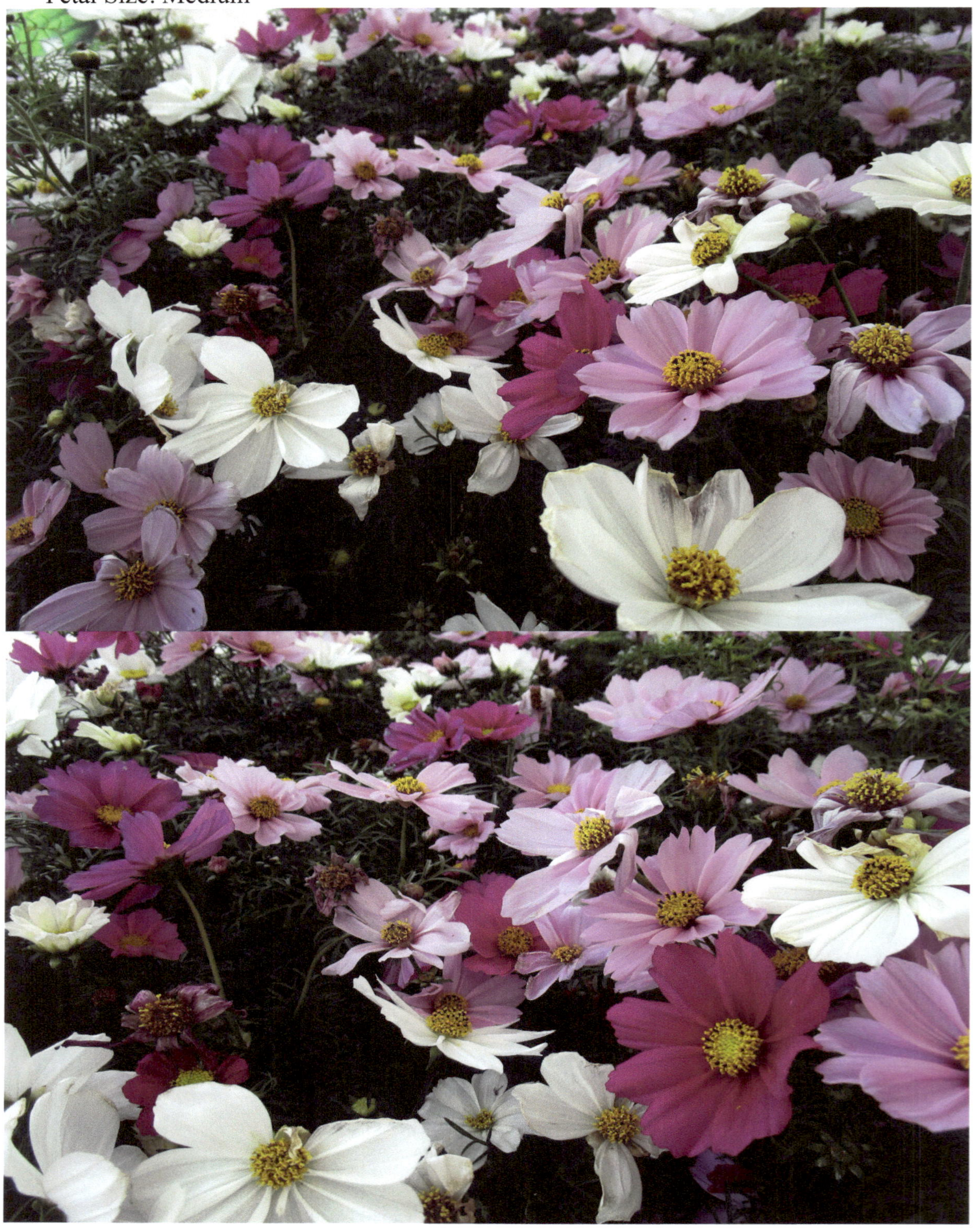

12. Crocus (Crocus tommasinianus)
    Colour: White; Purple; Violet; Yellow; Orange(Stamen)
    First Bloom: March
    Amount of Sun Needed: Moderate
    Scent: None
    Petal Size: Medium

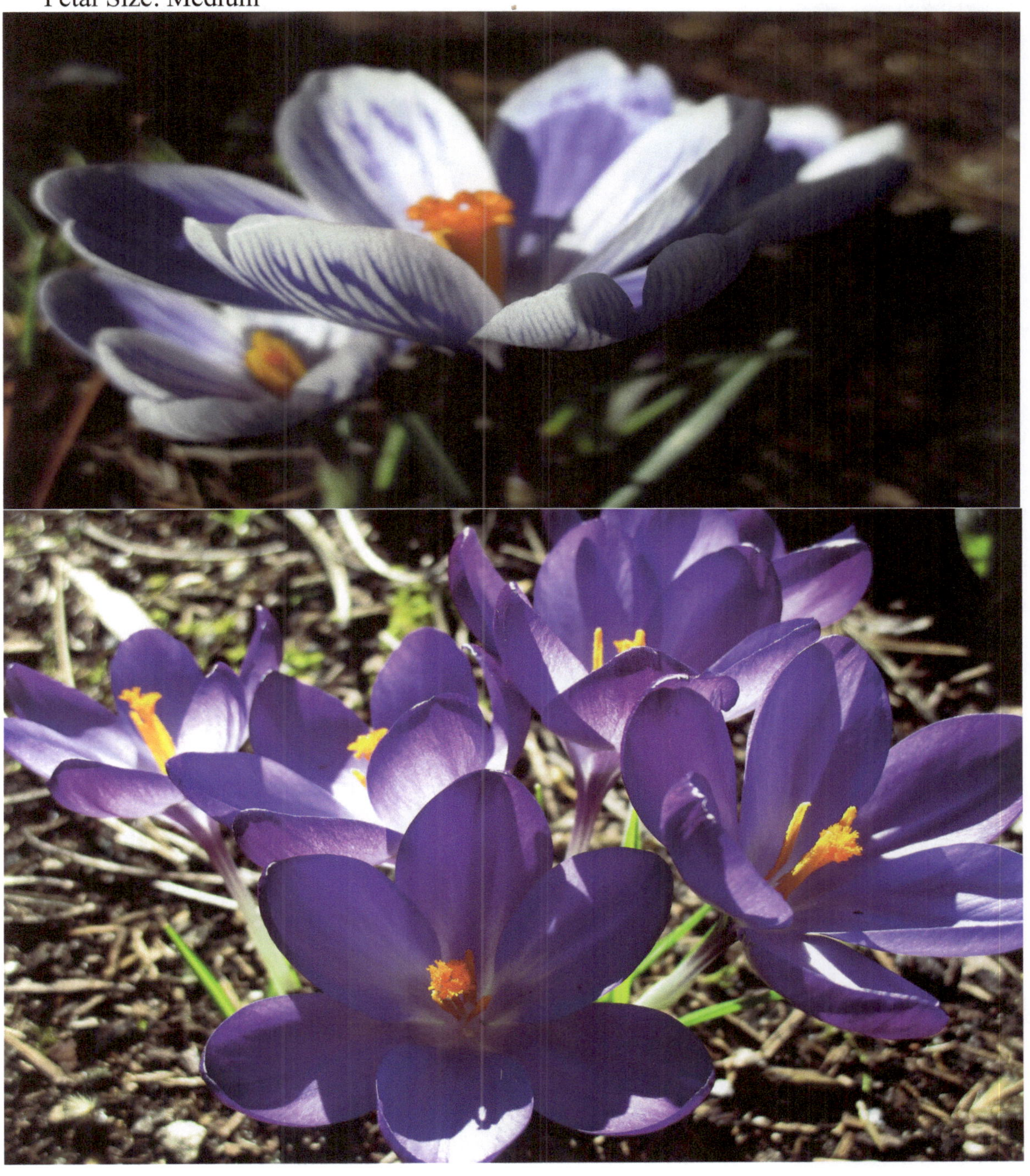

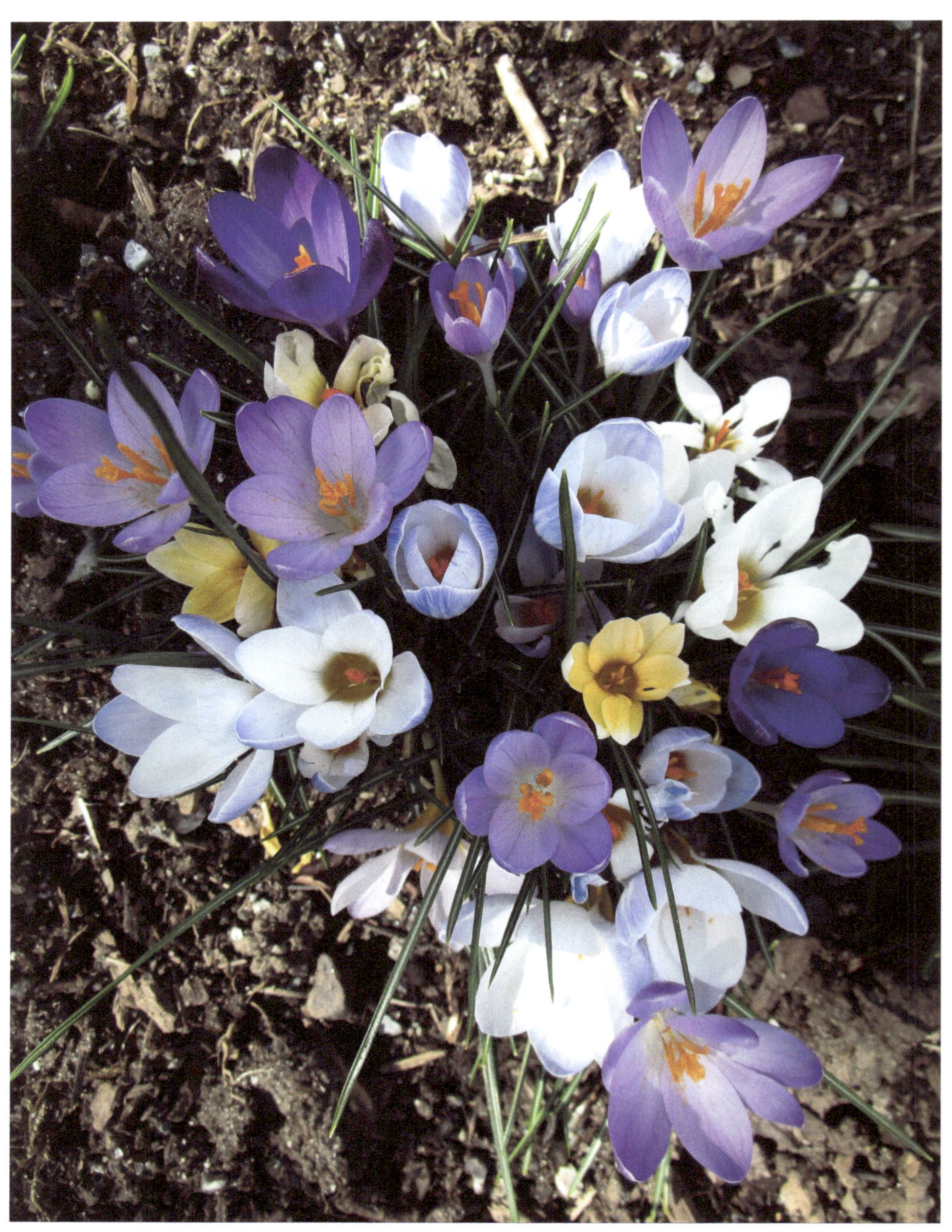

13. Daffodil (Narcissus)
   Colour: Yellow; Orange; White
   First Bloom: Early April
   Amount of Sun Needed: Moderate
   Scent: None
   Petal Size: Medium

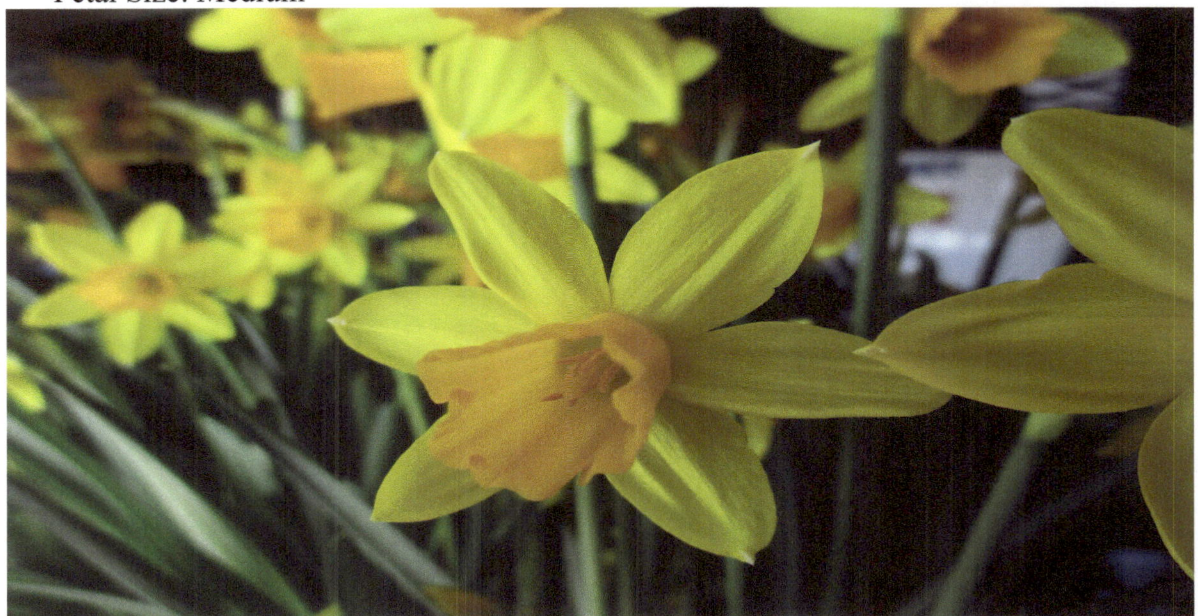

14. Dogwood (Cornus florida)
   Colour: Pink; White; Green
   First Bloom: June
   Scent: None
   Petal Size: Medium

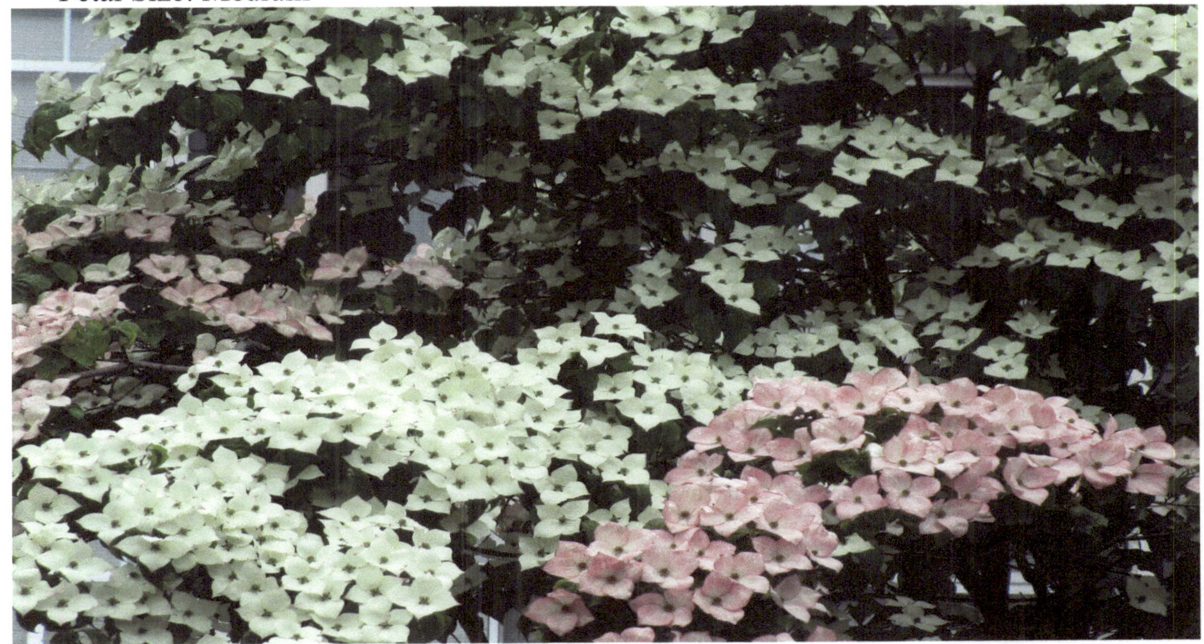

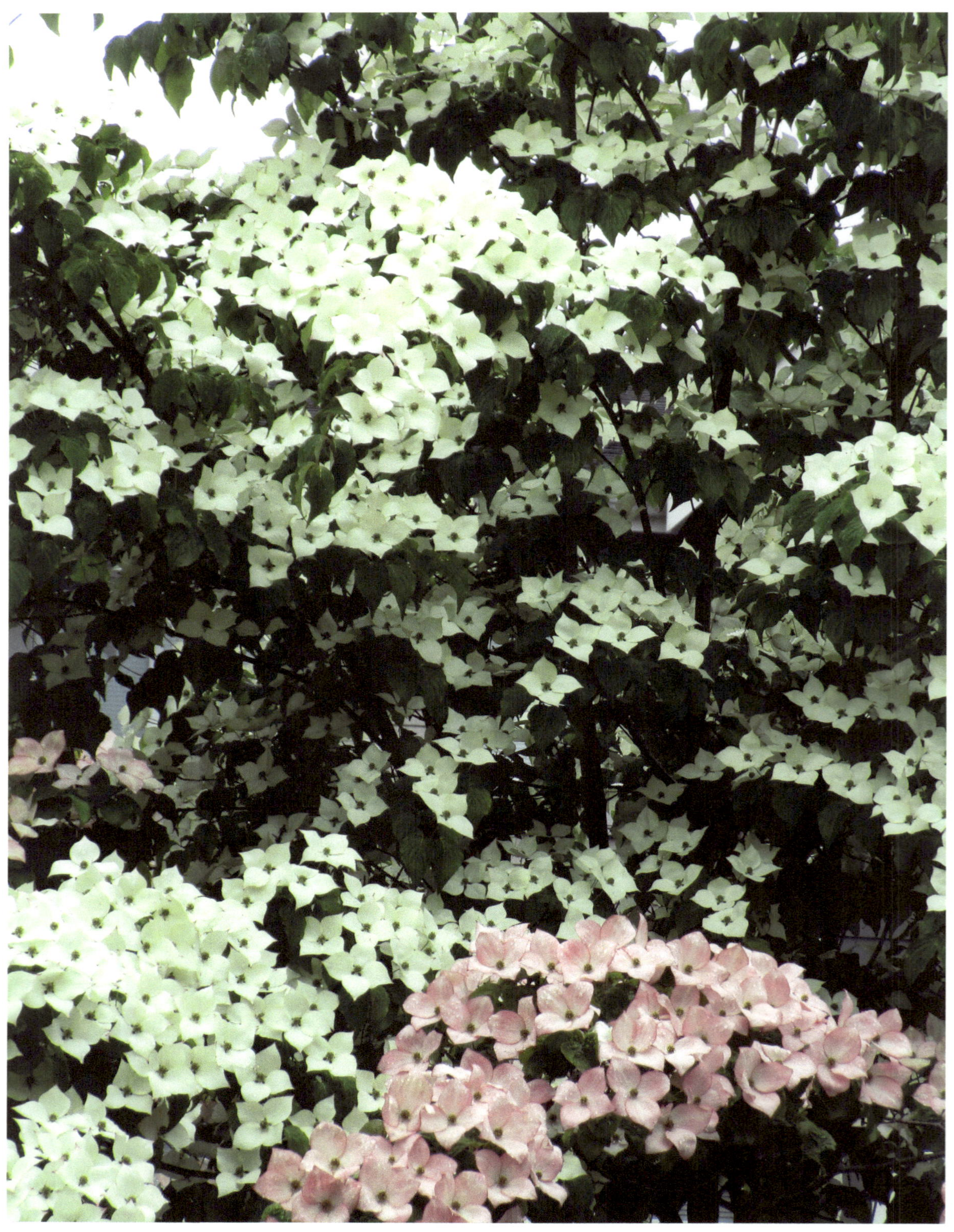

15. Forget-Me-Not (Myosotis)
    Colour: Blue; Pink; Purple; White; Yellow
    First Bloom: Mid-April
    Amount of Sun Needed: Moderate
    Scent: None
    Petal Size: Small

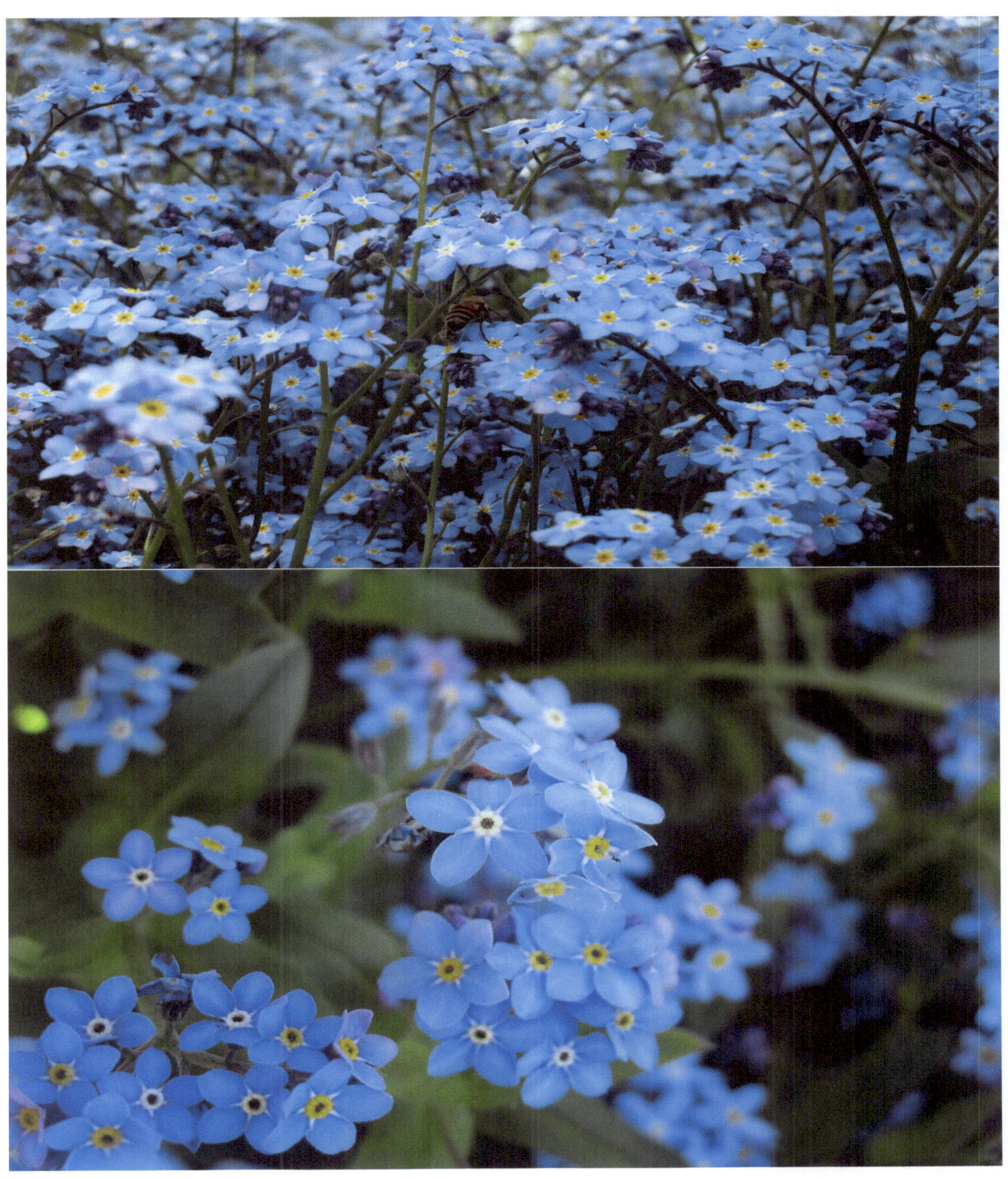

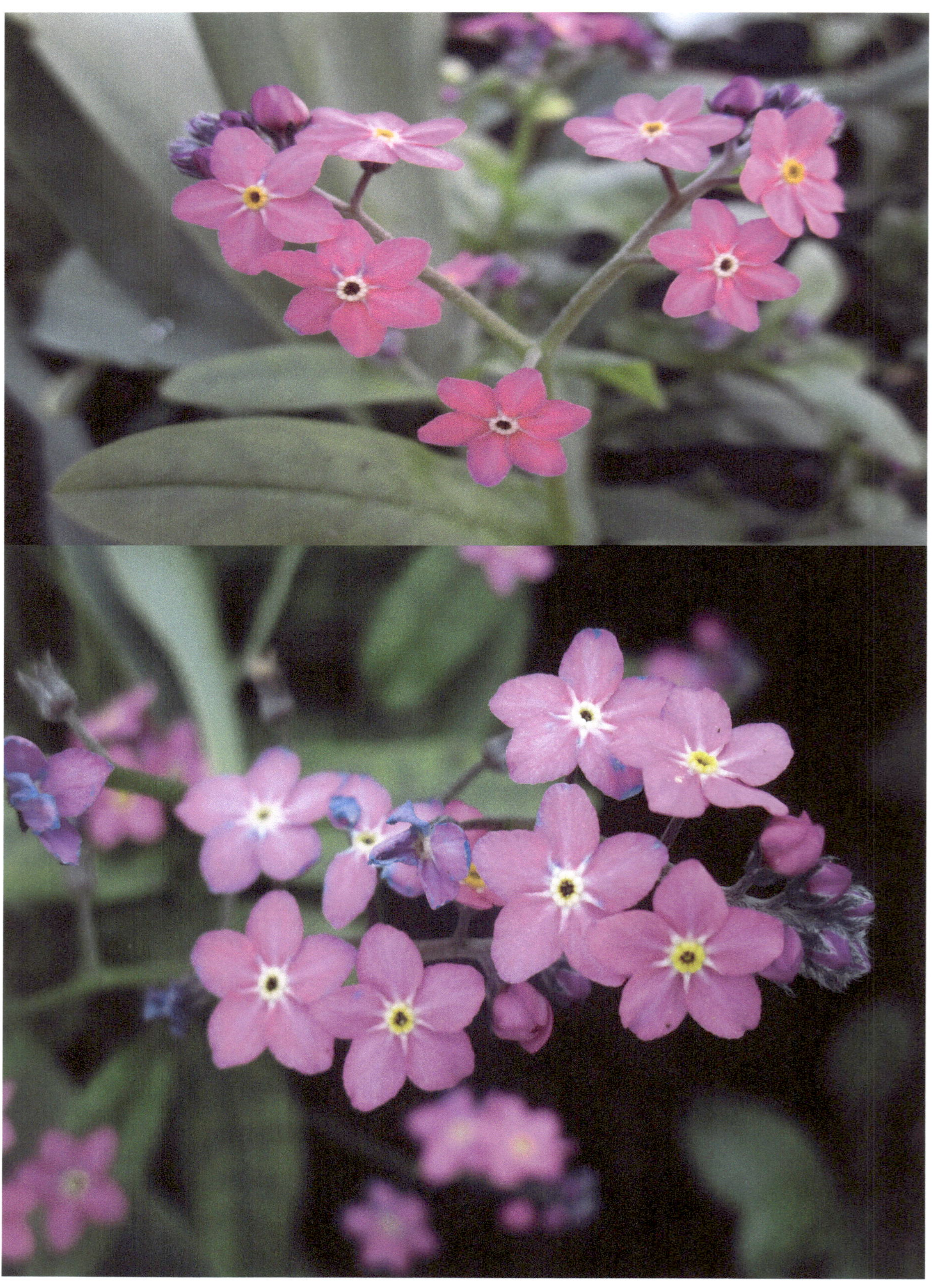

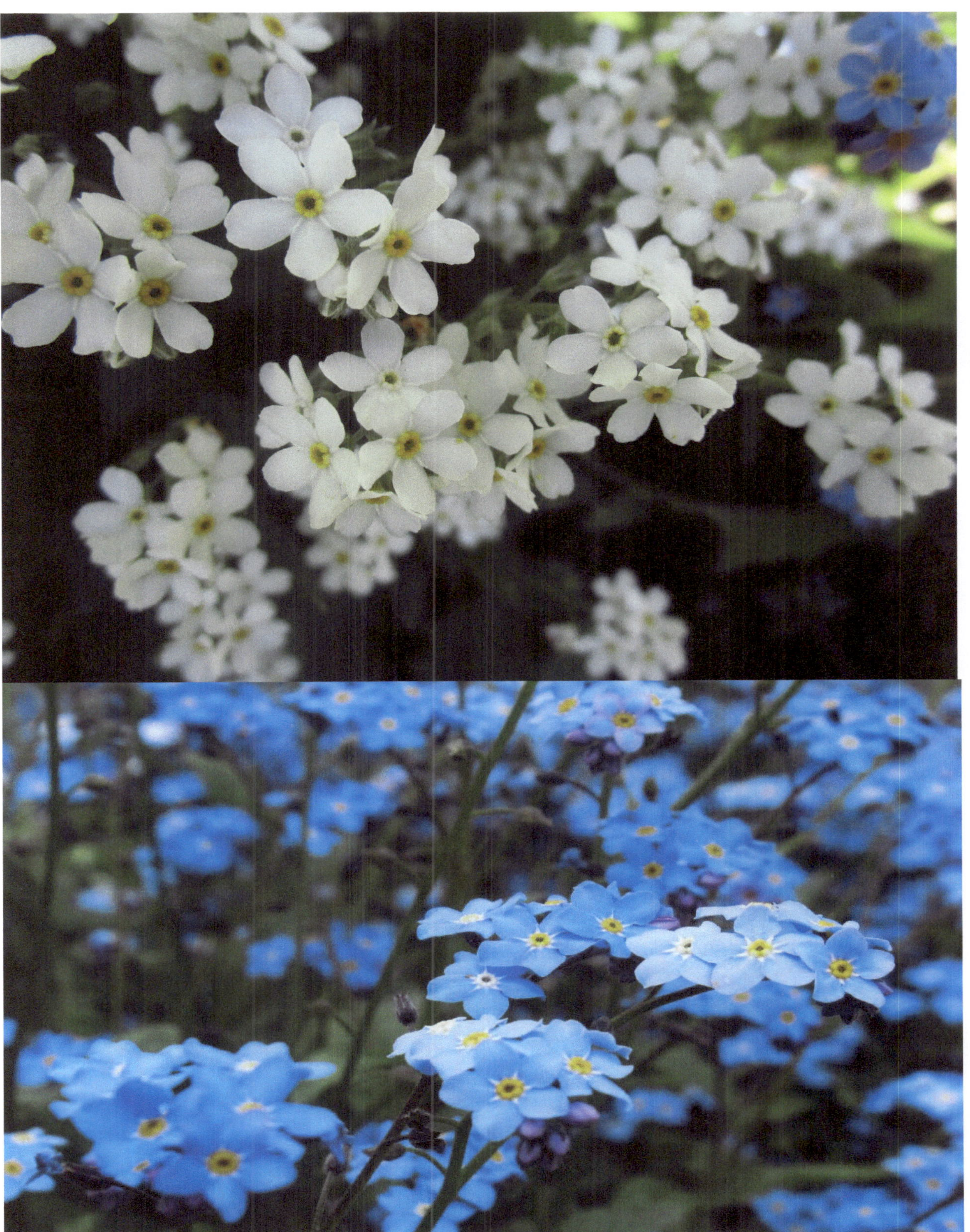

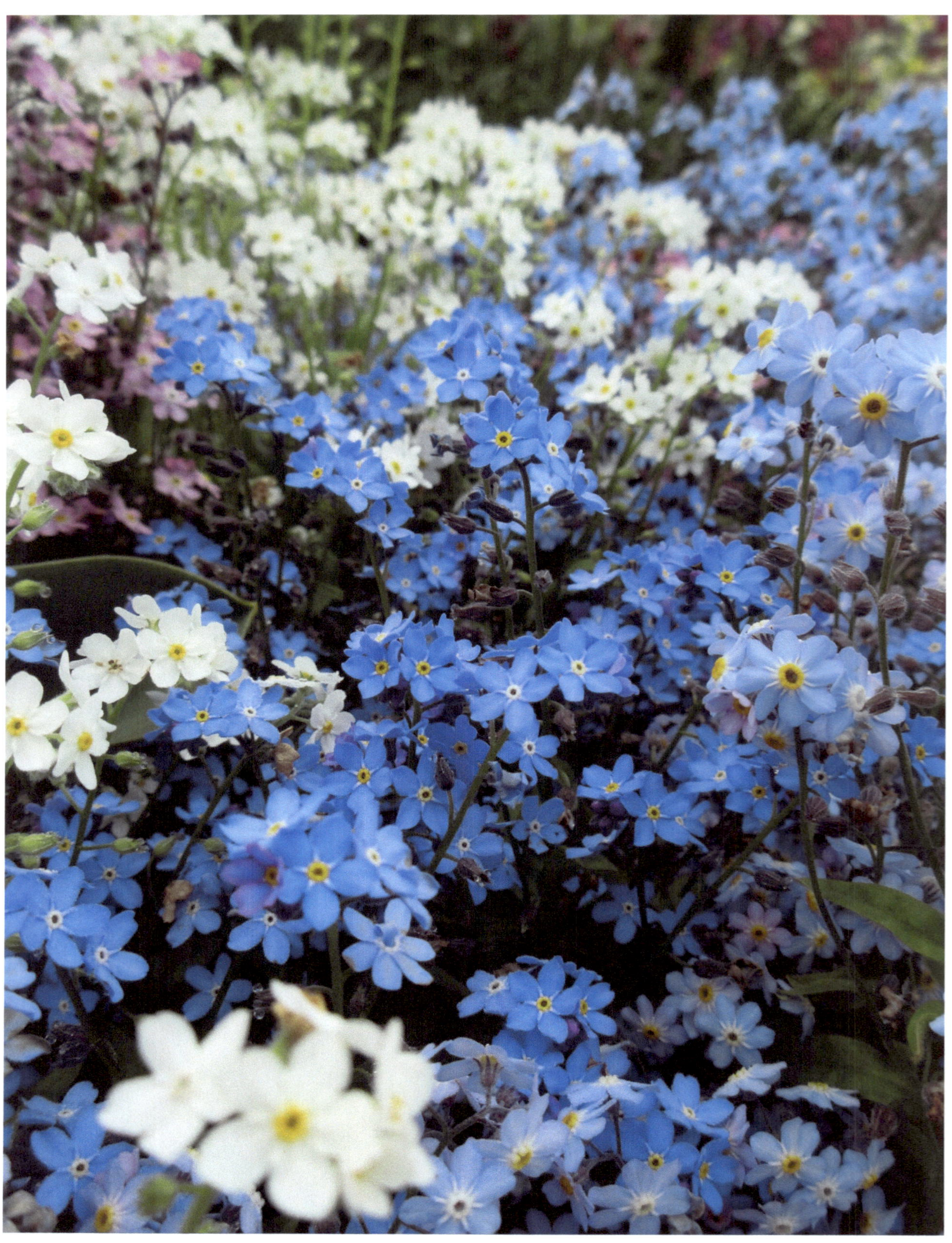

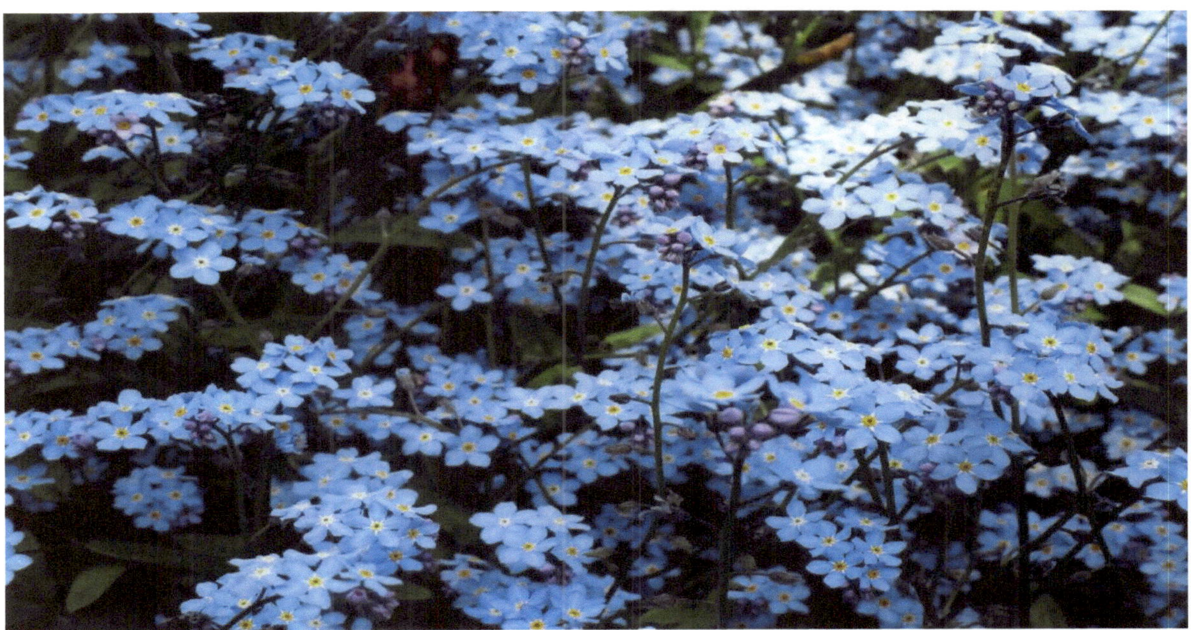

16. French Hollyhock (Malva sylvestris)
    Colour: Purple; Blue; White; Violet; Varied
    First Bloom: May
    Amount of Sun Needed: Mild
    Scent: None
    Petal Size: Fairly Medium

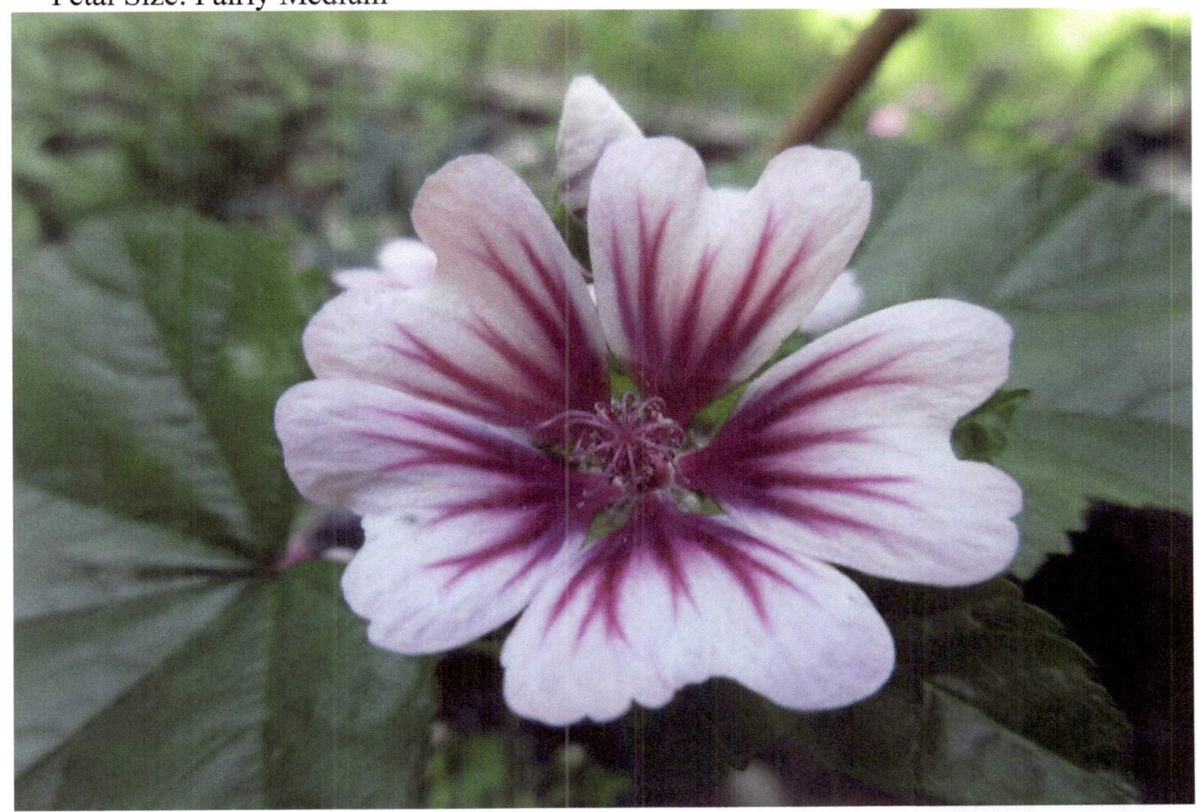

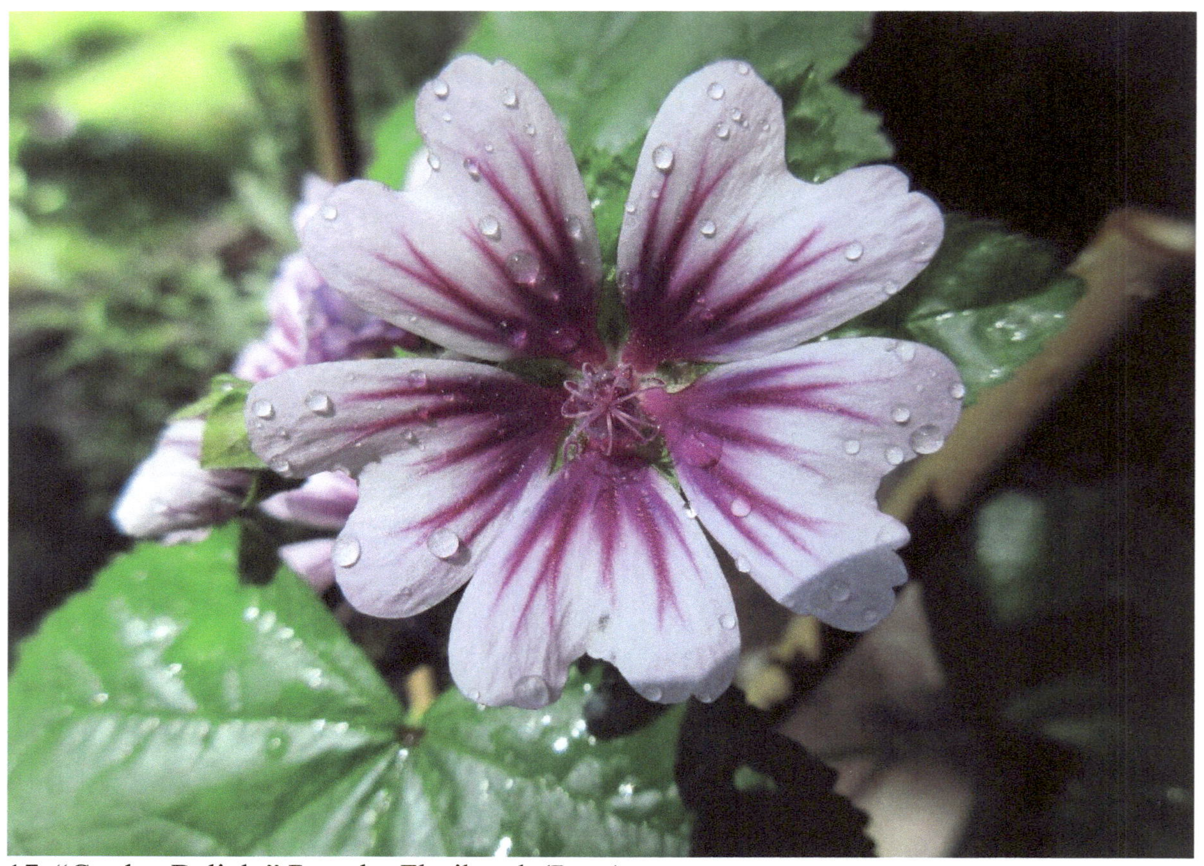

17. "Garden Delight" Rose by Floribunda(Rosa)
   Colour: Pink; Peach; Red; White; Yellow; Orange; Varied
   First Bloom: June
   Amount of Sun Needed: Moderate to Full
   Scent: None
   Petal Size: Medium to Fairly Large

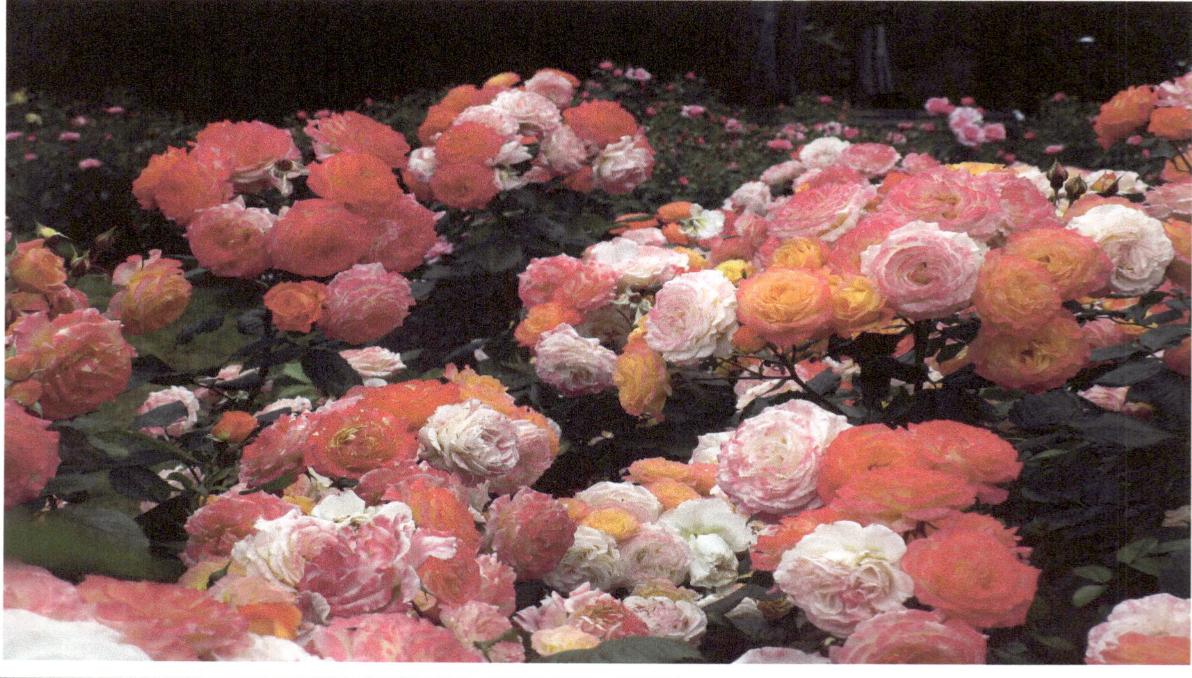

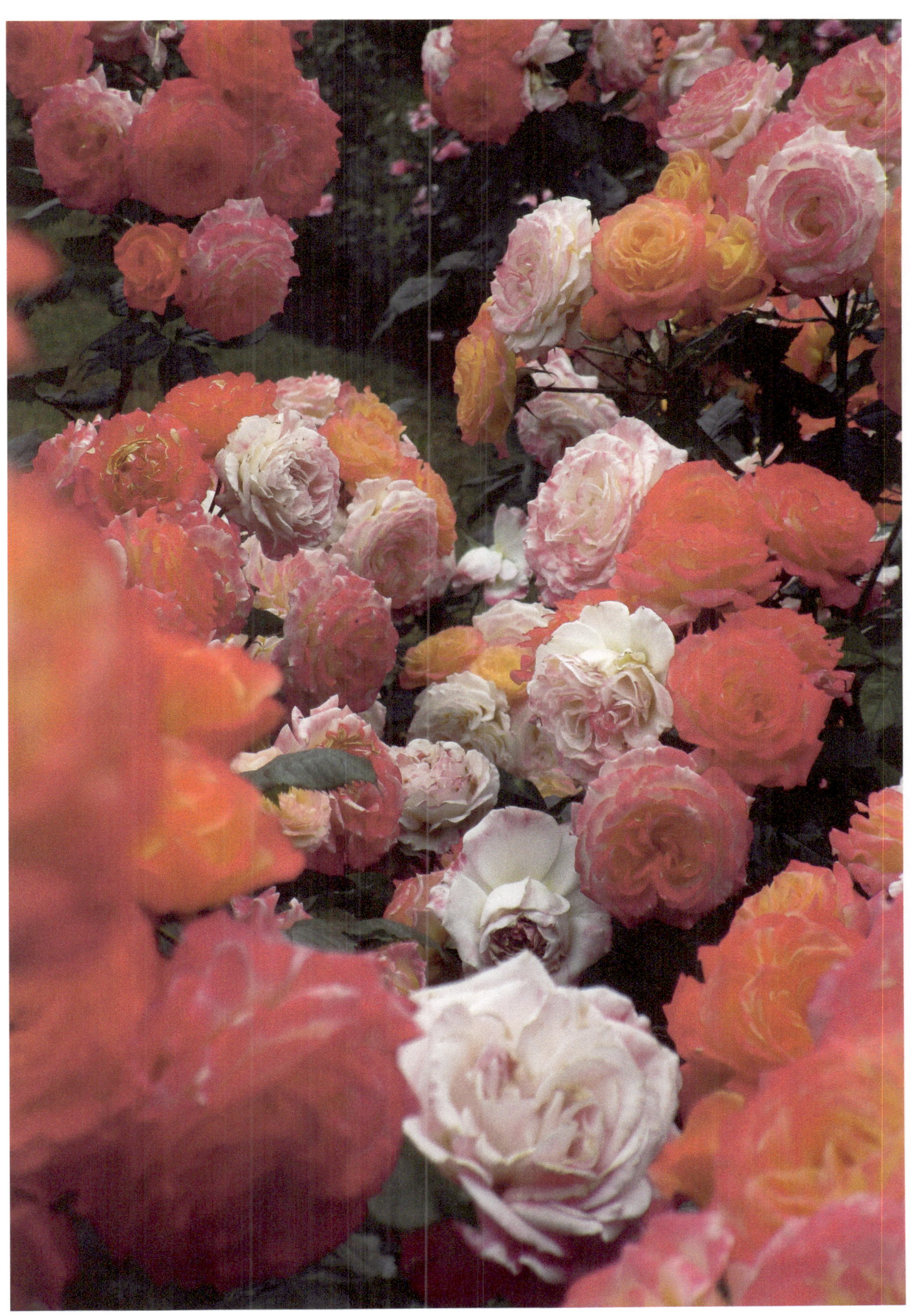

18. Geranium (Pelargonium)
    Colour: Pink; White; Red; Varied
    First Bloom: April
    Amount of Sun Needed: Mild
    Scent: None
    Petal Size: Medium

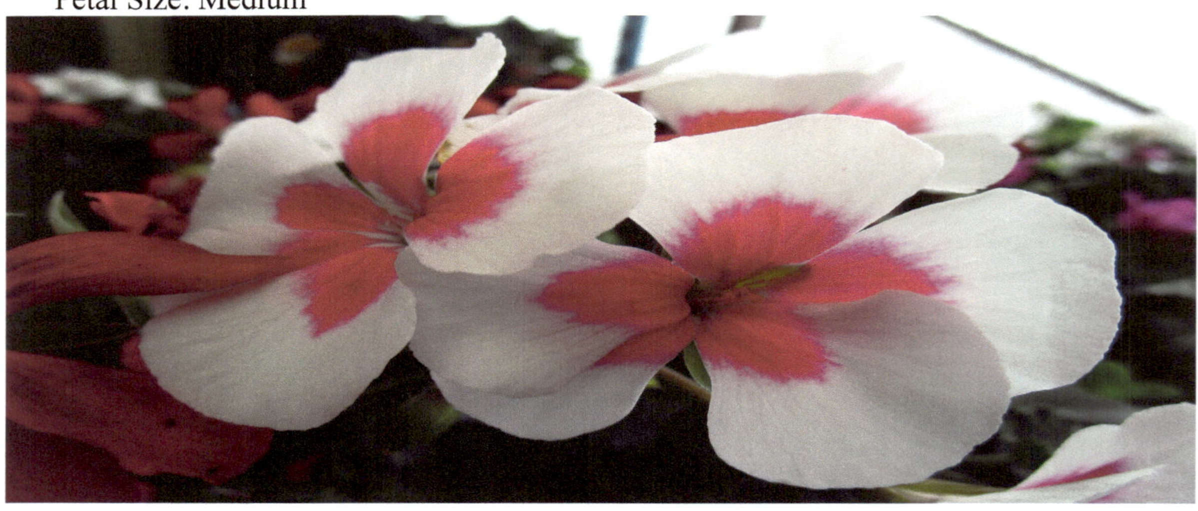

19. Grape Hyacinth (Muscari)
    Colour: Blue
    First Bloom:
    Amount of Sun Needed: Moderate to Full
    Scent: None
    Petal Size: Small(Bulb-like)

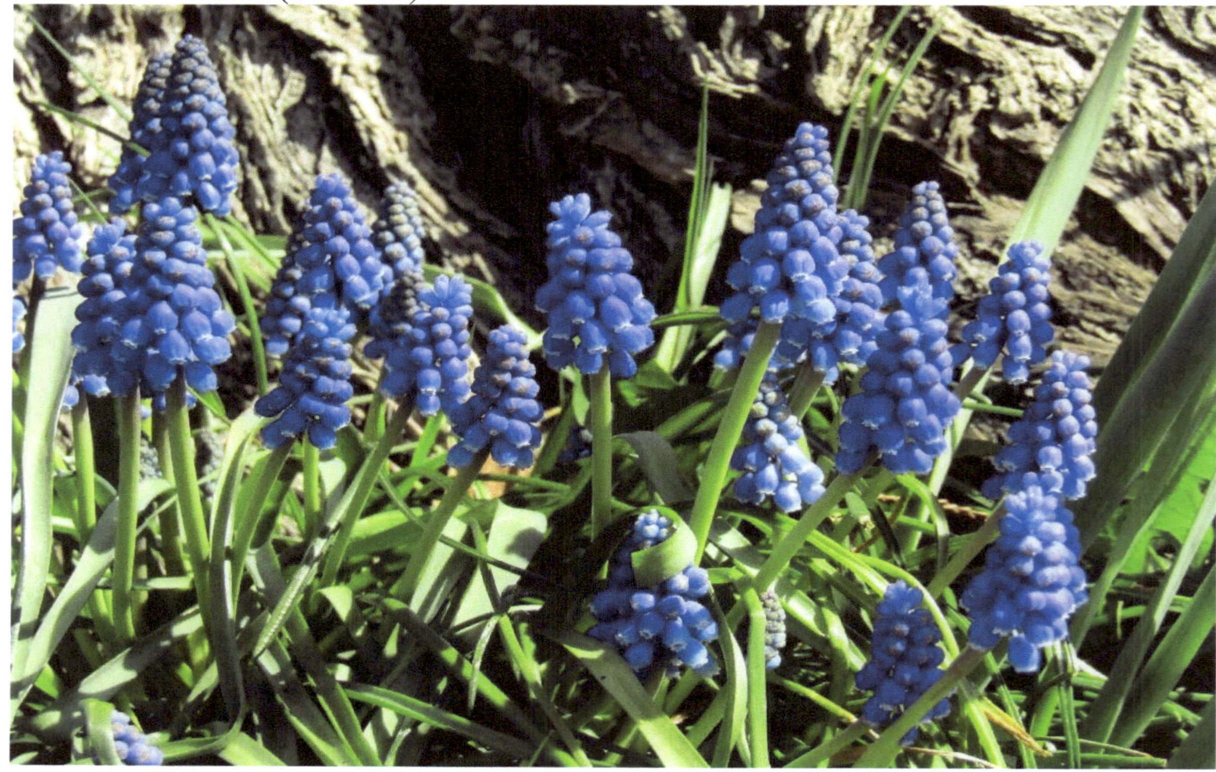

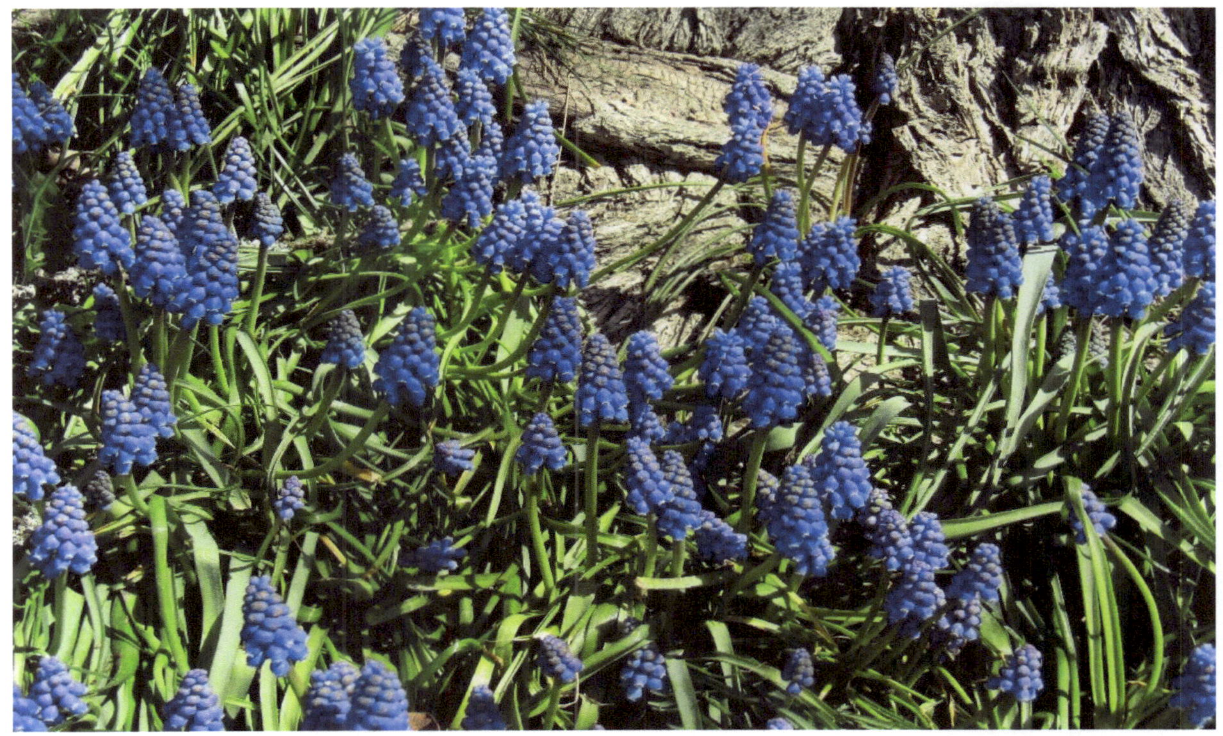

20. Grecian Windflower (Anemone Blanda)
    Colour: Blue; Violet; White; Yellow(Centre)
    First Bloom:
    Amount of Sun Needed: Mild to Moderate
    Scent: None
    Petal Size: Fairly Medium

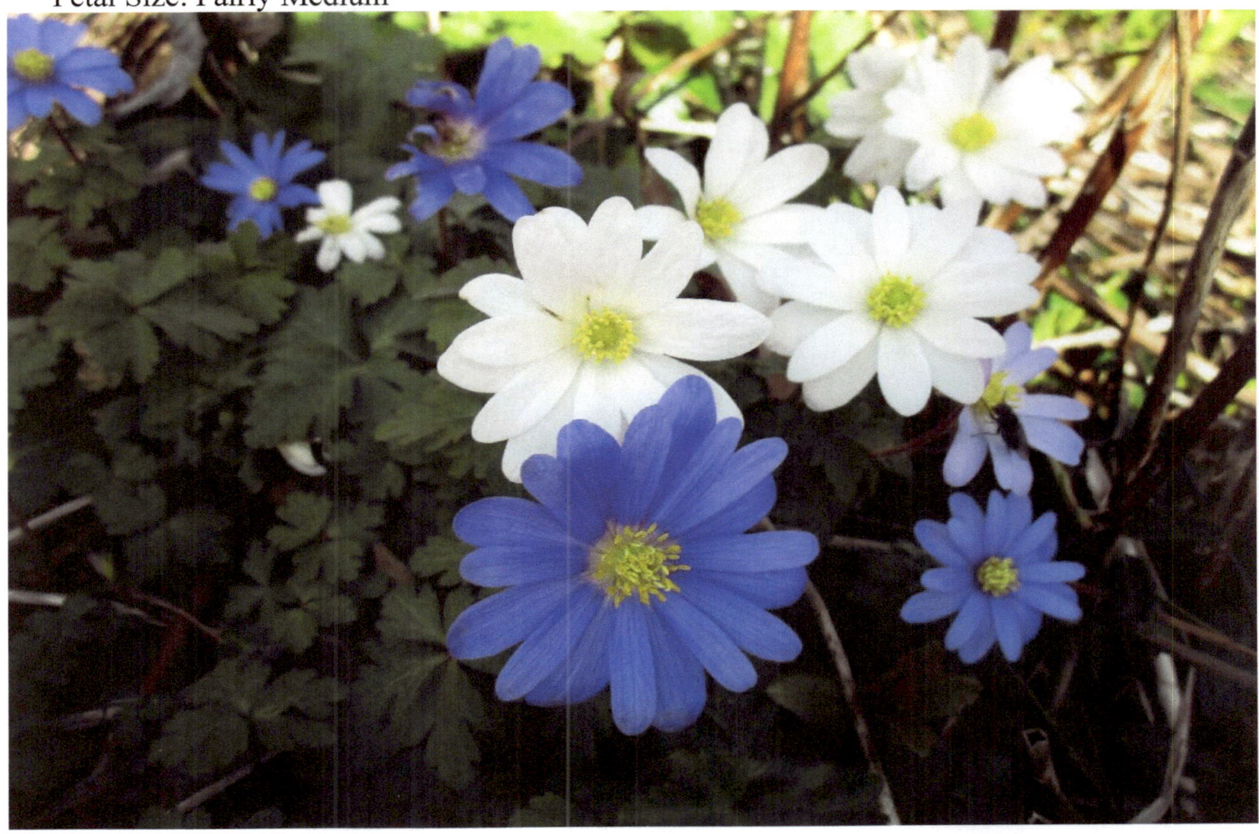

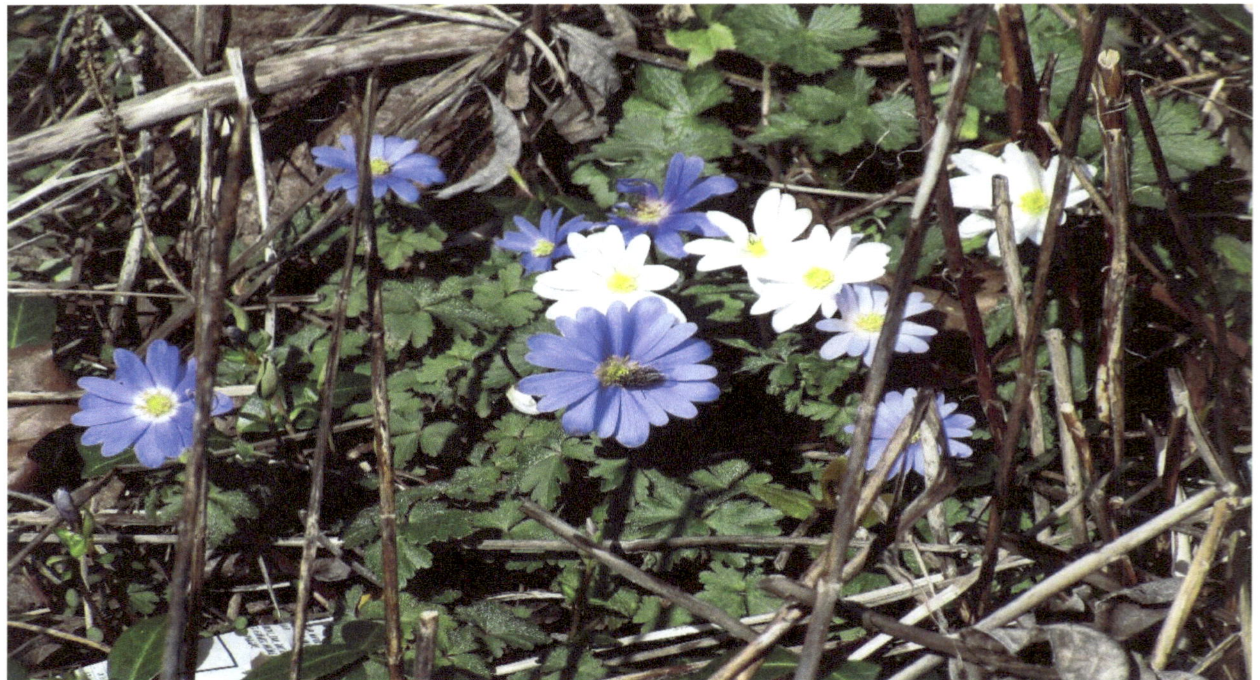

21. Hydrangea (Hydrangea)
   Colour: Blue; Pink; White; Red; Varied
   First Bloom: May
   Amount of Sun Needed: Moderate to Full
   Scent: None
   Petal Size: Small to Moderate

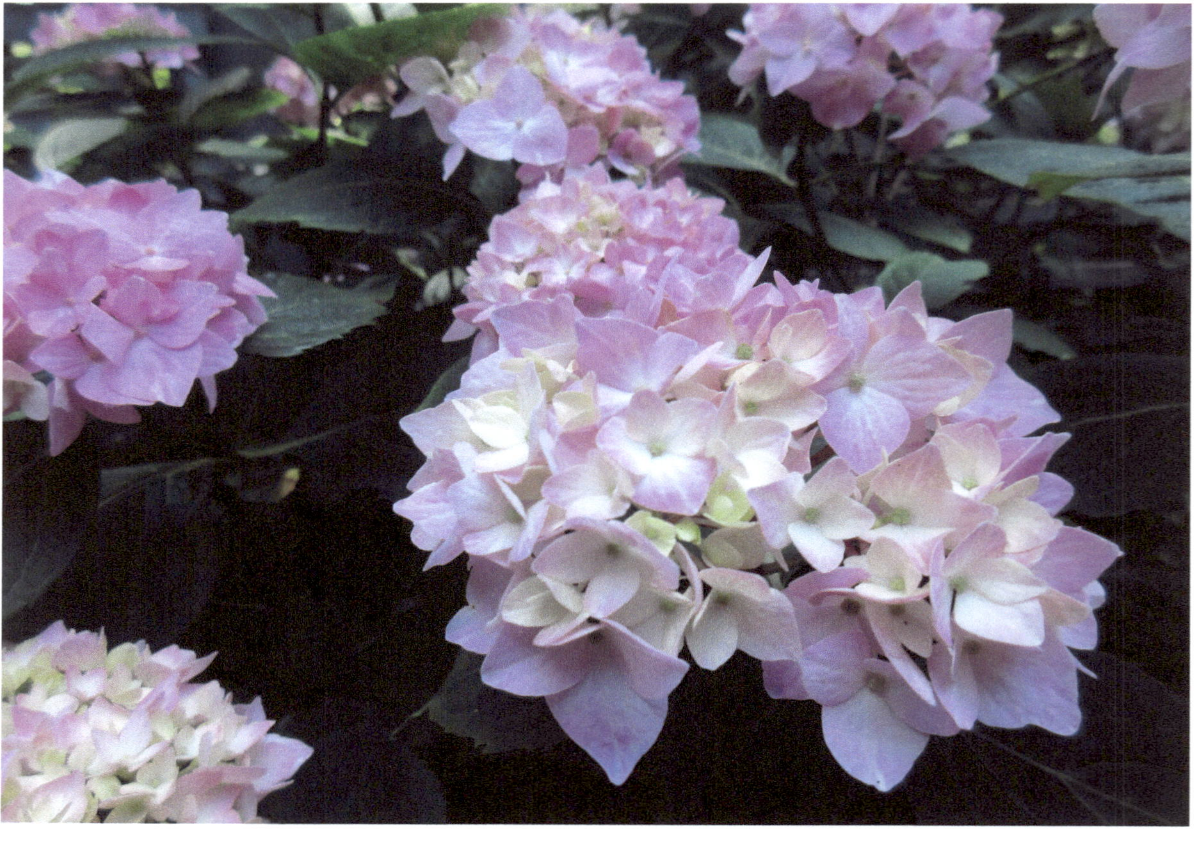

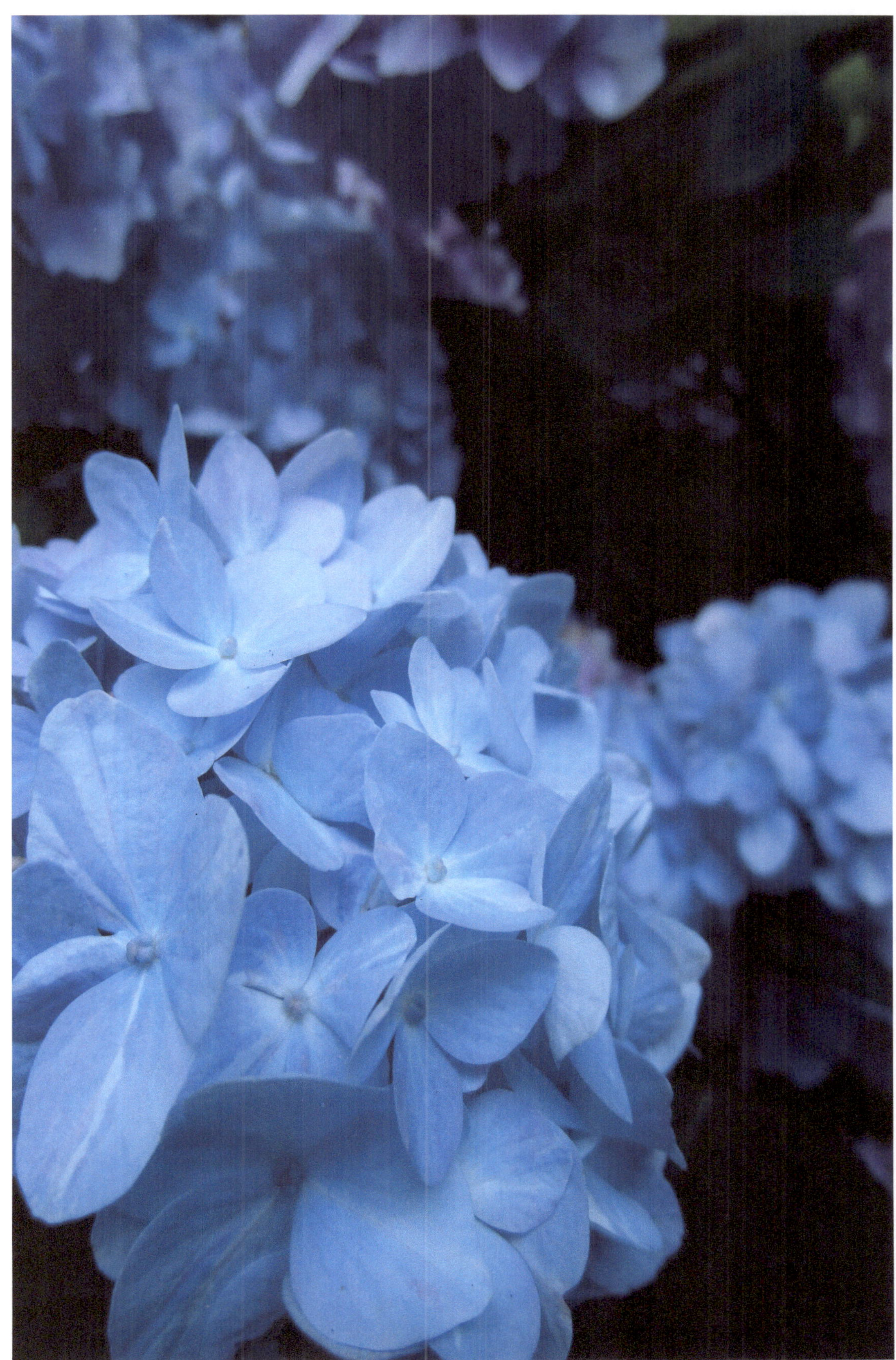

22. Huntington Carpet Rosemary (Rosmarinus officinalis)
    Colour: Light Blue; White
    First Bloom: April
    Amount of Sun Needed: Mild
    Scent: Mild
    Petal Size: Small

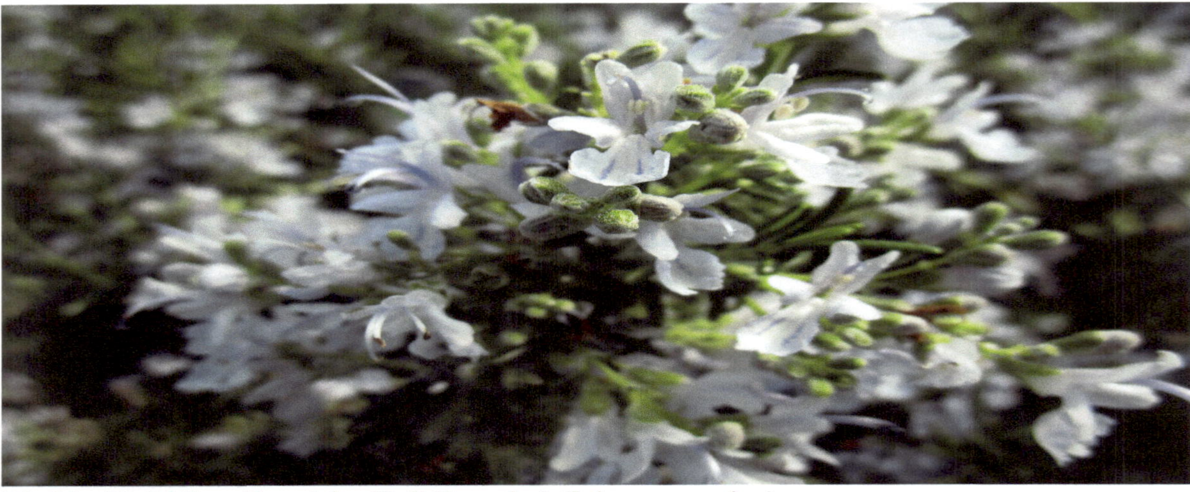

23. Iris **'Babbling Brook' – Tall Bearded (Iris germanica)**
    Colour: White; Sky Blue; Yellow
    First Bloom: May
    Amount of Sun Needed: Moderate to Full
    Scent: None
    Petal Size: Fairly Large

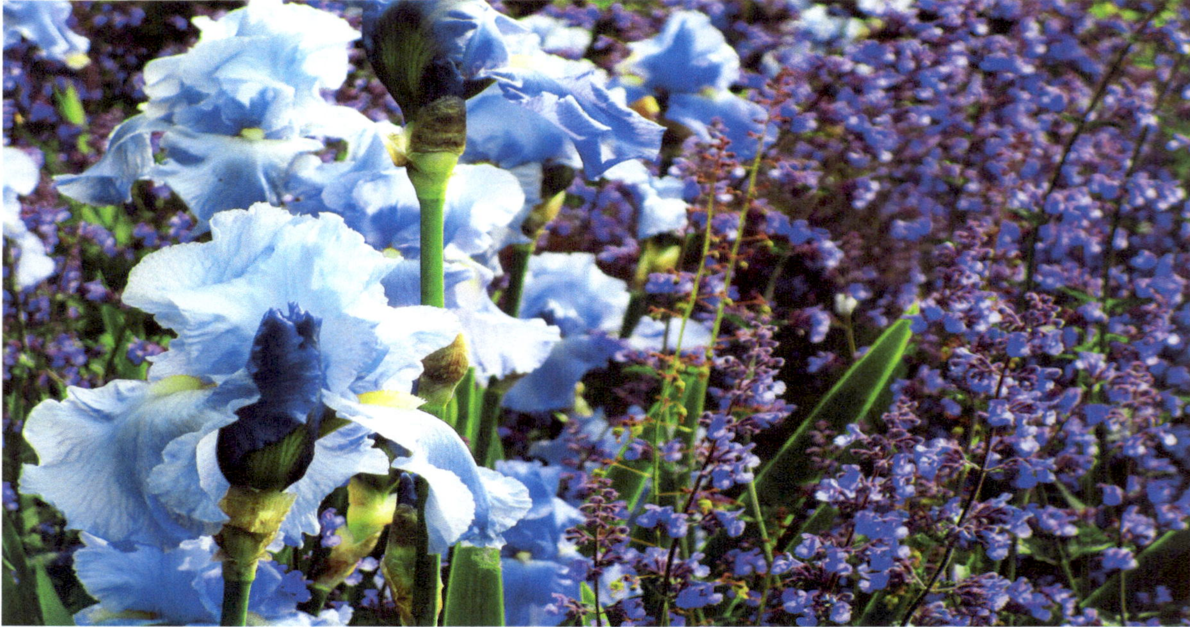

A source of inspiration for the traditional symbol of French royalty, irises have a stylised appearance of their petals that speaks of elegance and representation for the elite upper class. The combination of colours, like the stunning blue, white and yellow in these Iris **'Babbling Brook,' are particularly well-matched in hues that call for hopeful admiration and awe.**

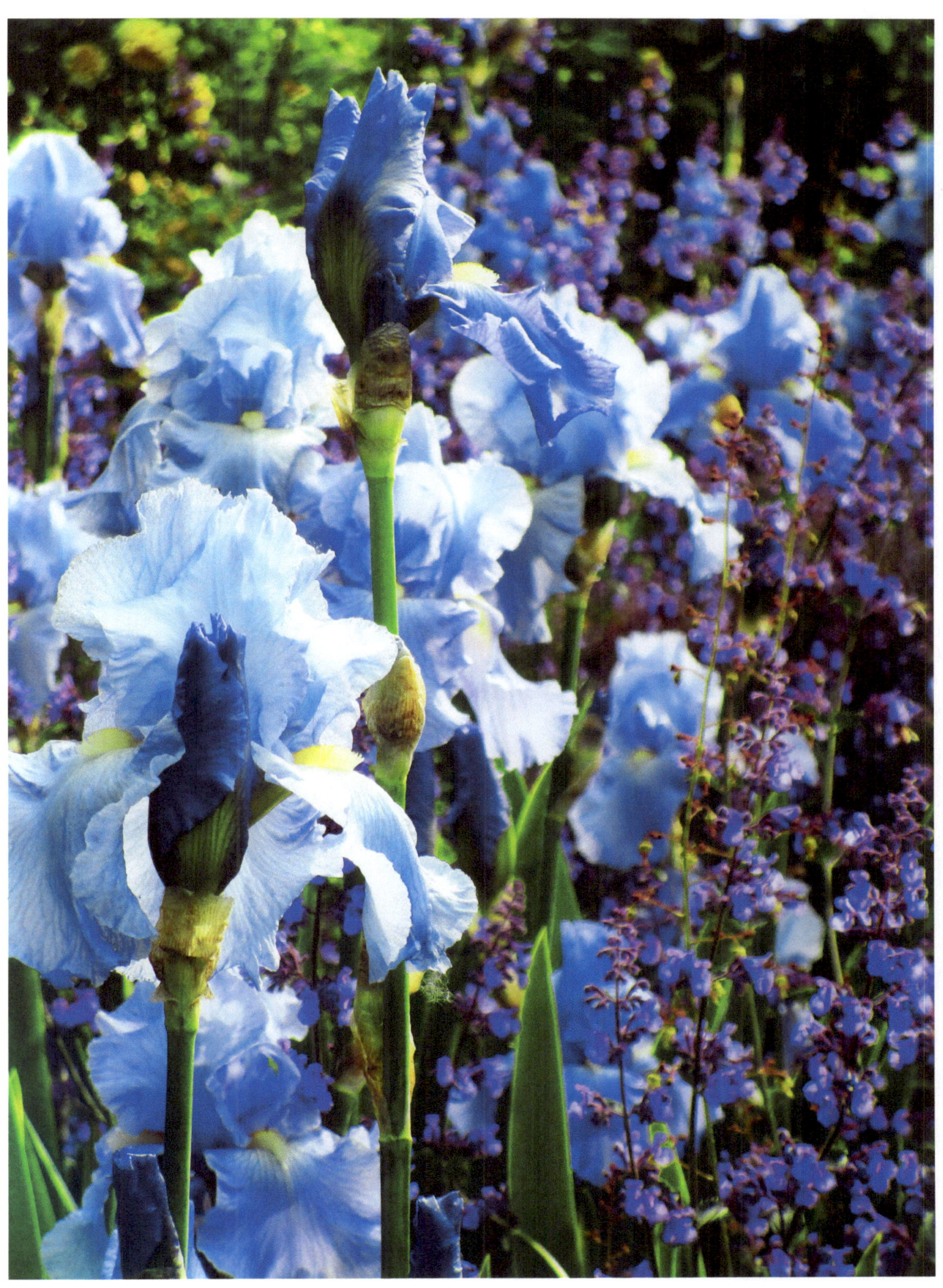

24. Kalanchoe (Kalanchoe blossfeldiana)
    Colour: Red; Pink; White; Varied
    First Bloom: March
    Amount of Sun Needed: Mild
    Scent: None
    Petal Size: Small

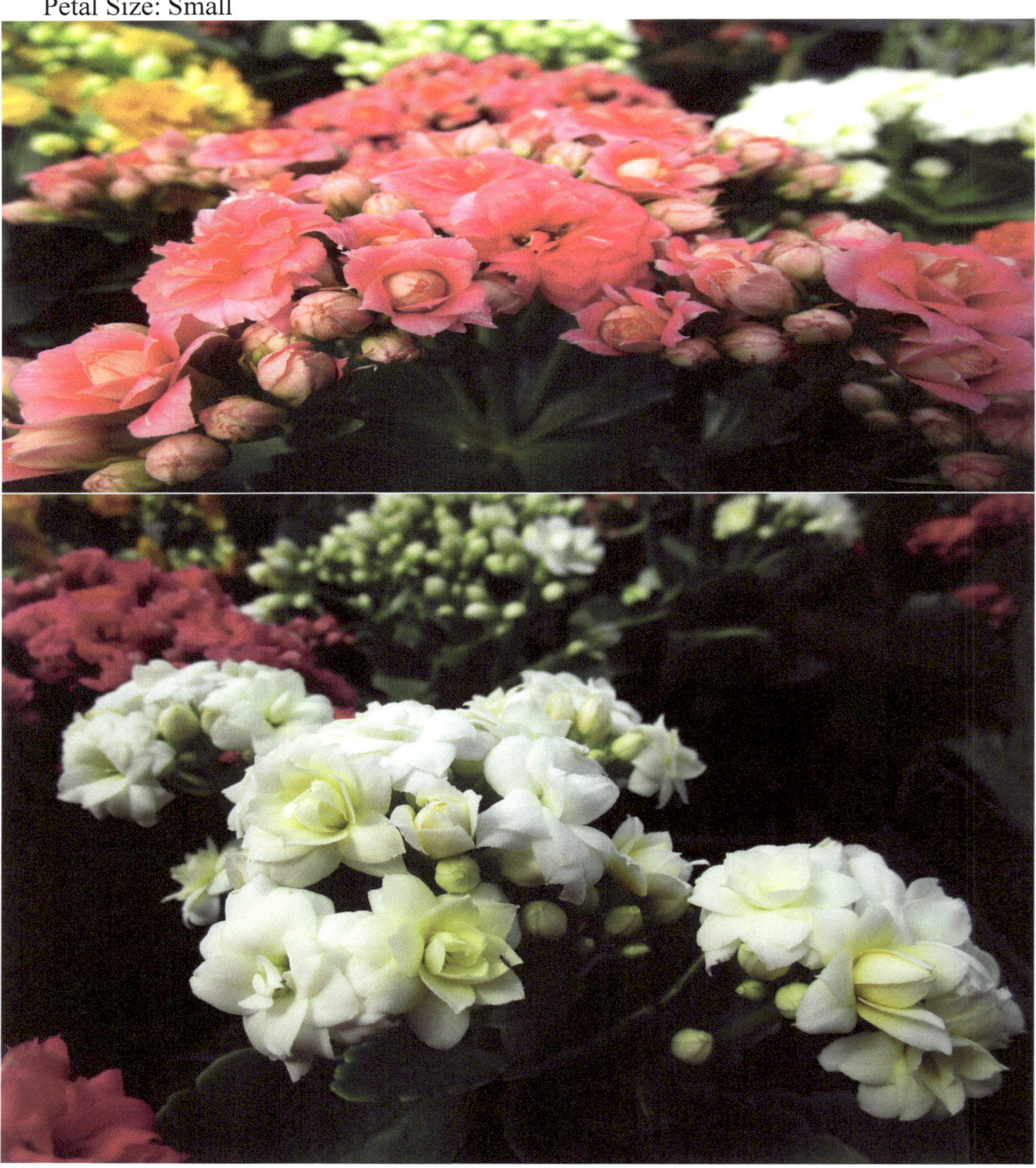

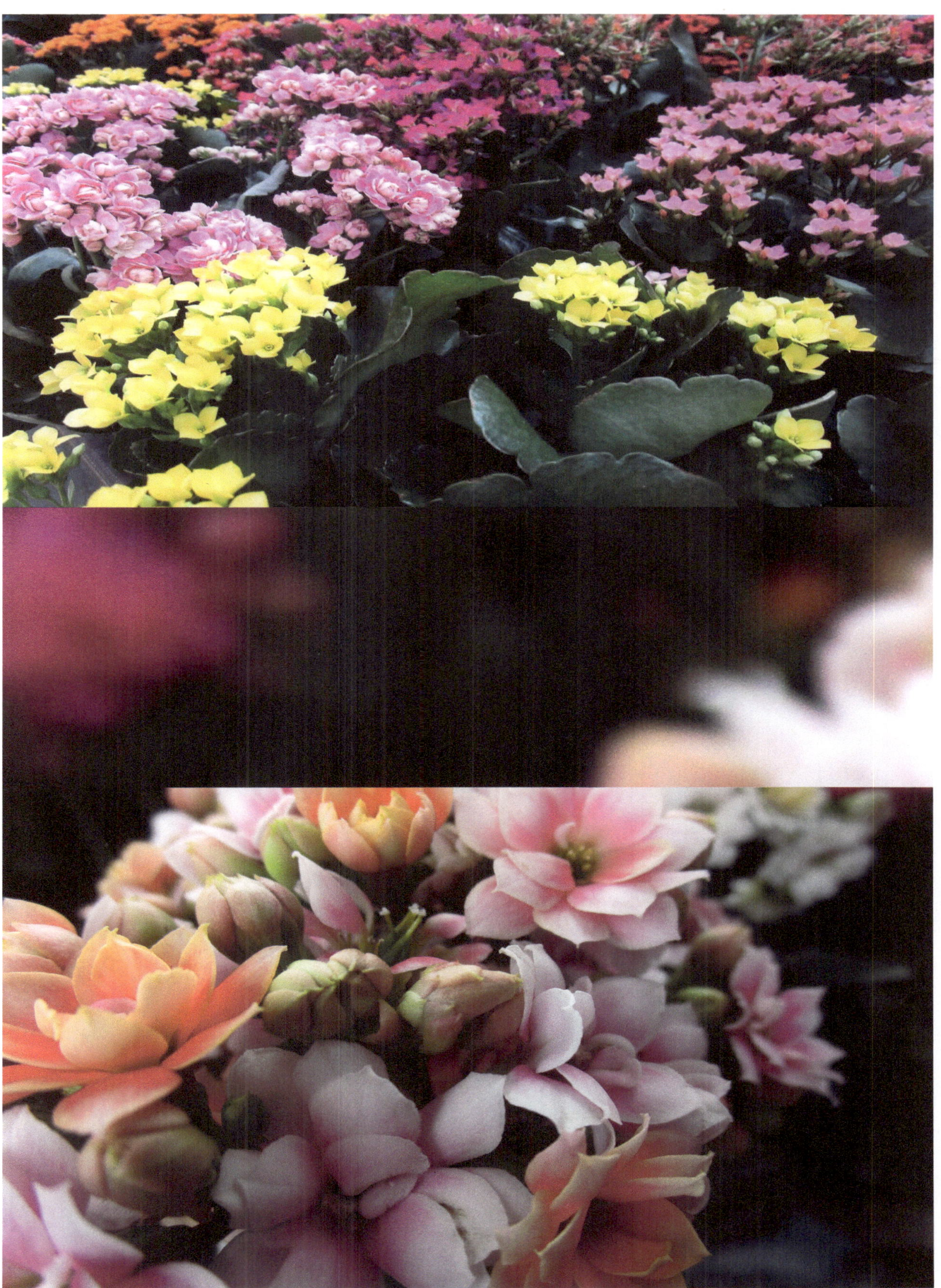

25. "Leander" English Rose by David Austin (Rosa)
   Colour: Apricot; Light Peach; White
   First Bloom: June
   Amount of Sun Needed: Moderate to Full
   Scent: None
   Petal Size: Medium

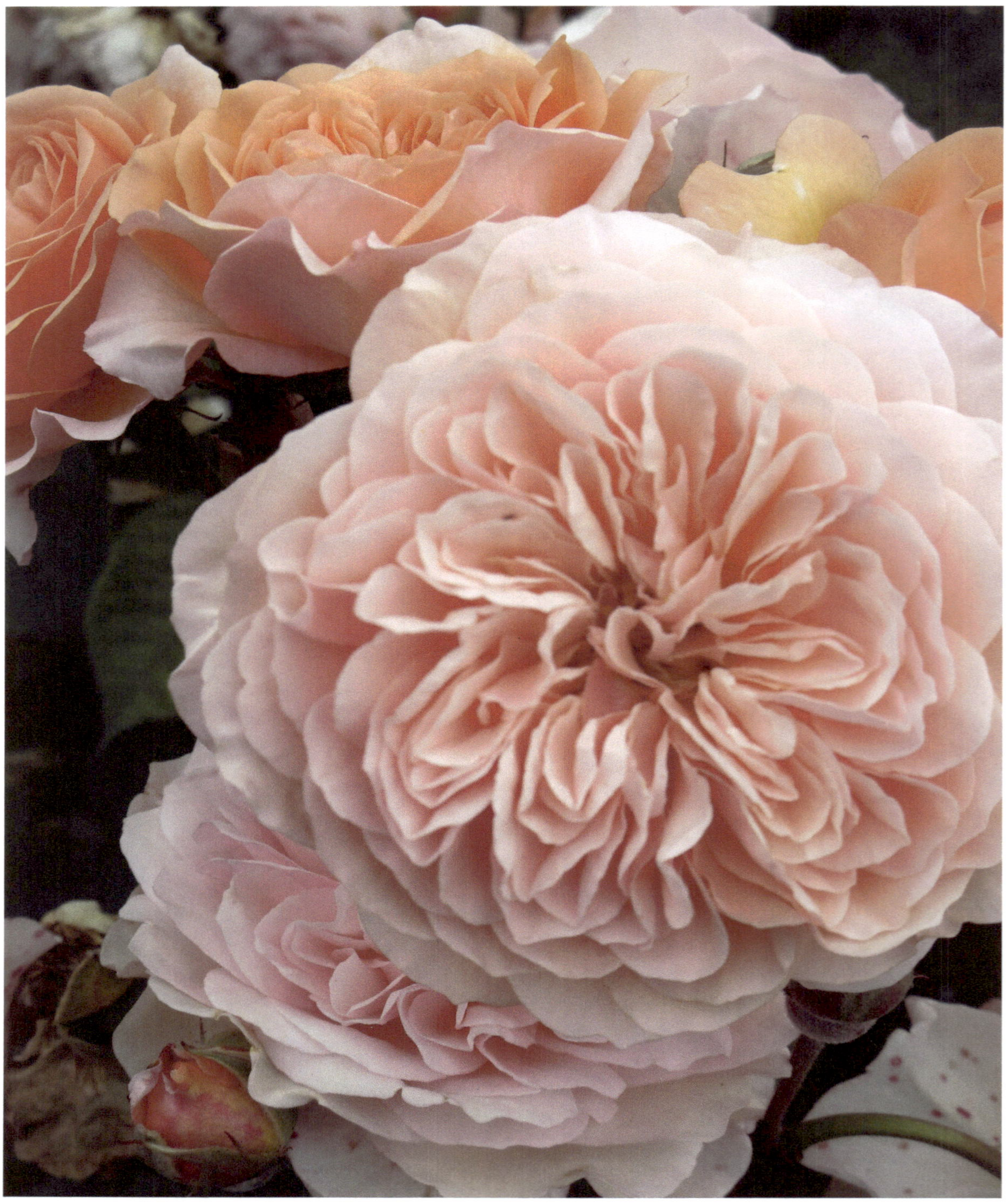

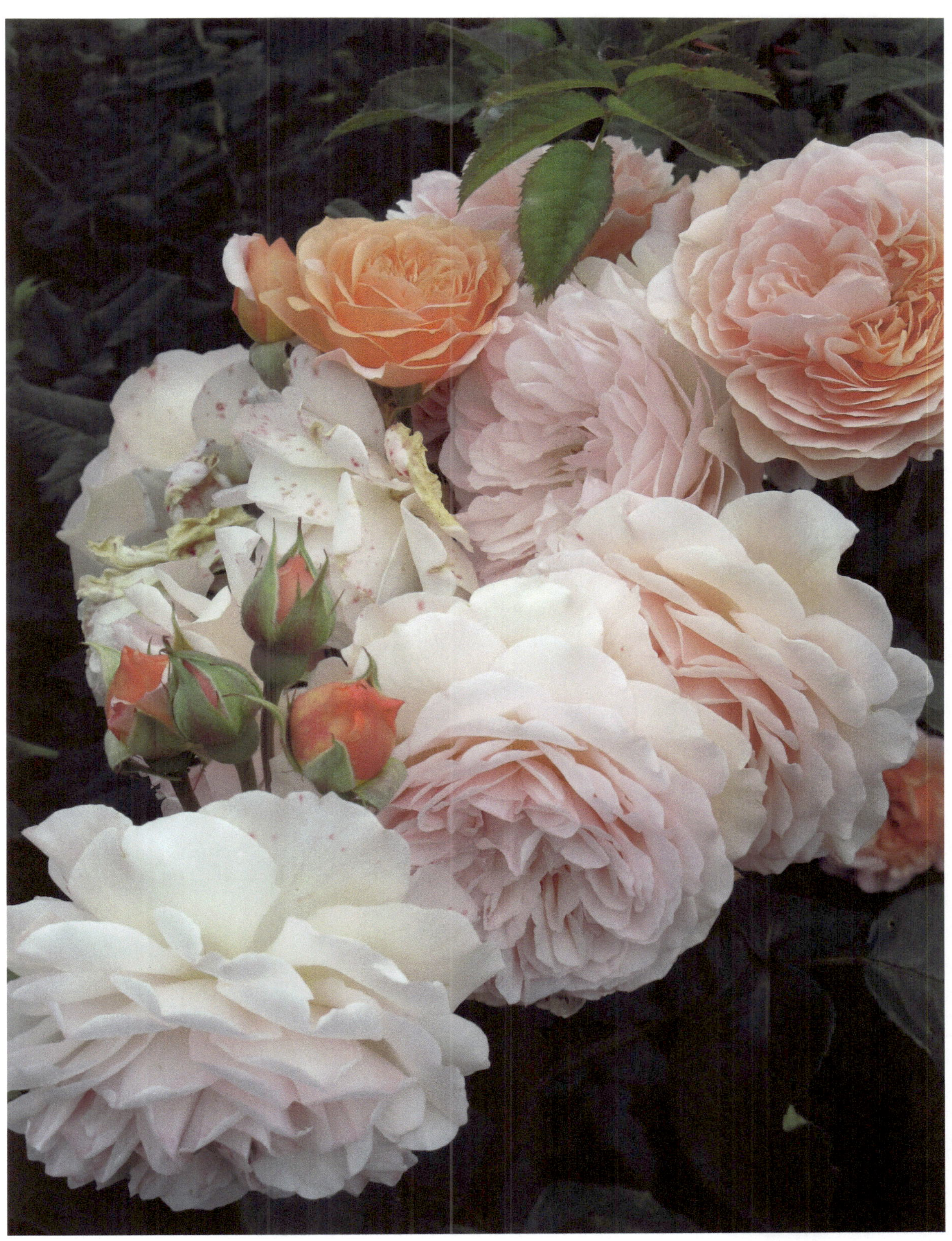

26. Lily (Lilium)
    Colour: White; Pink; Red; Yellow; Varied
    First Bloom: Late April to Early May
    Amount of Sun Needed: Moderate
    Scent: Mild to Strong
    Petal Size: Medium to Large

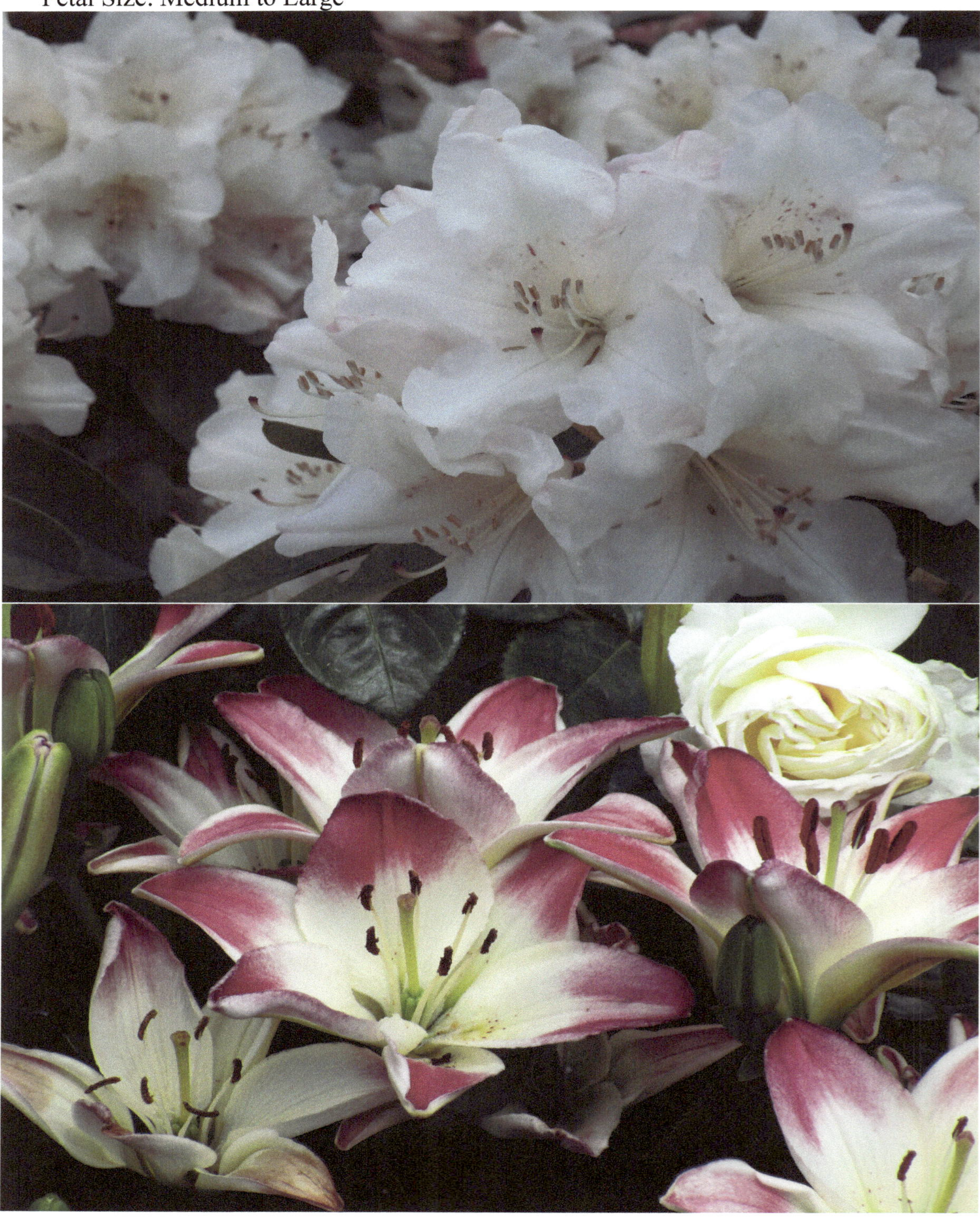

27. Lupine
   Colour: Purple; Violet; Yellow; Green; Varied
   First Bloom: May
   Amount of Sun Needed: Full
   Scent: Mild
   Petal Size: Small to Fairly Medium

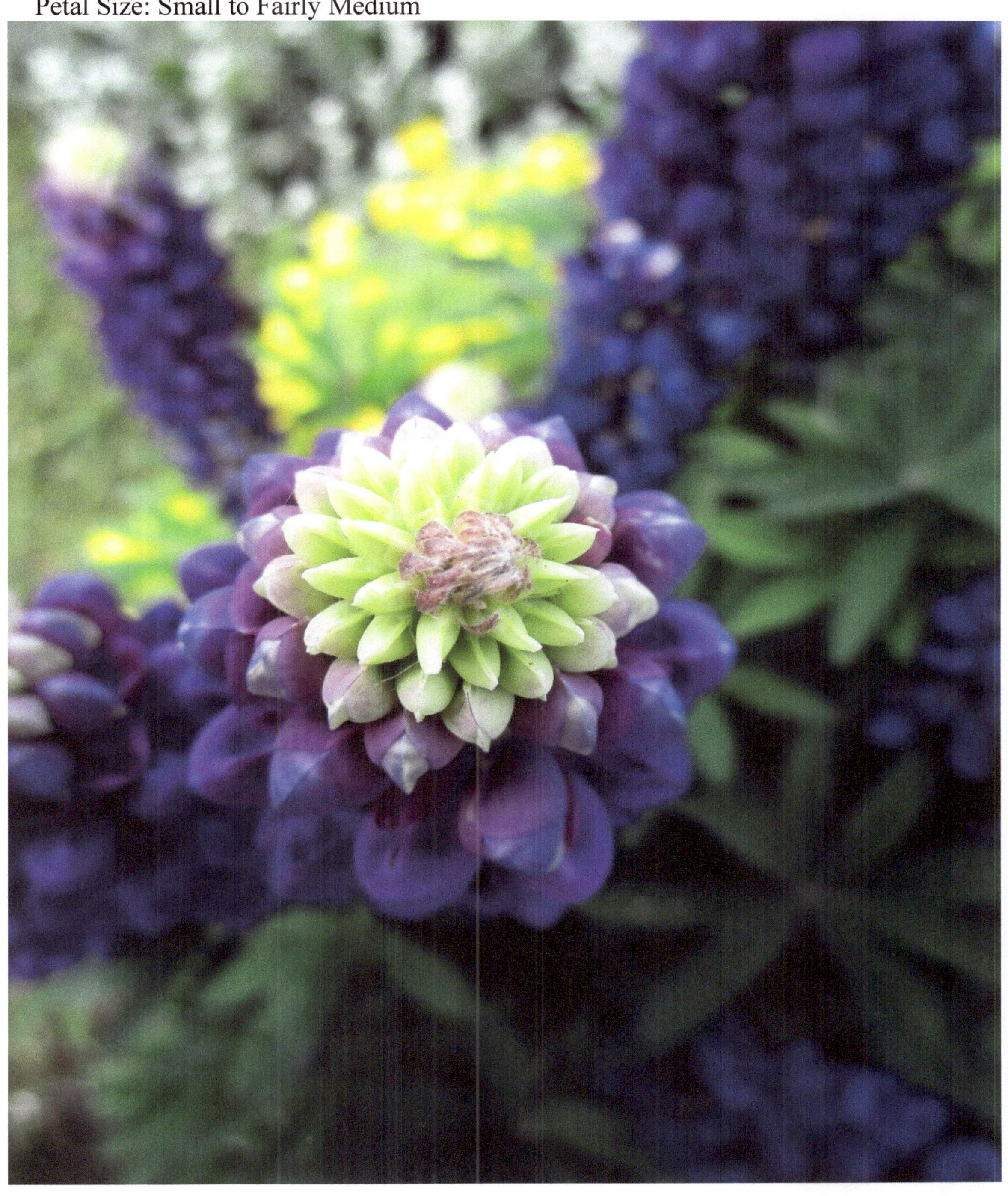

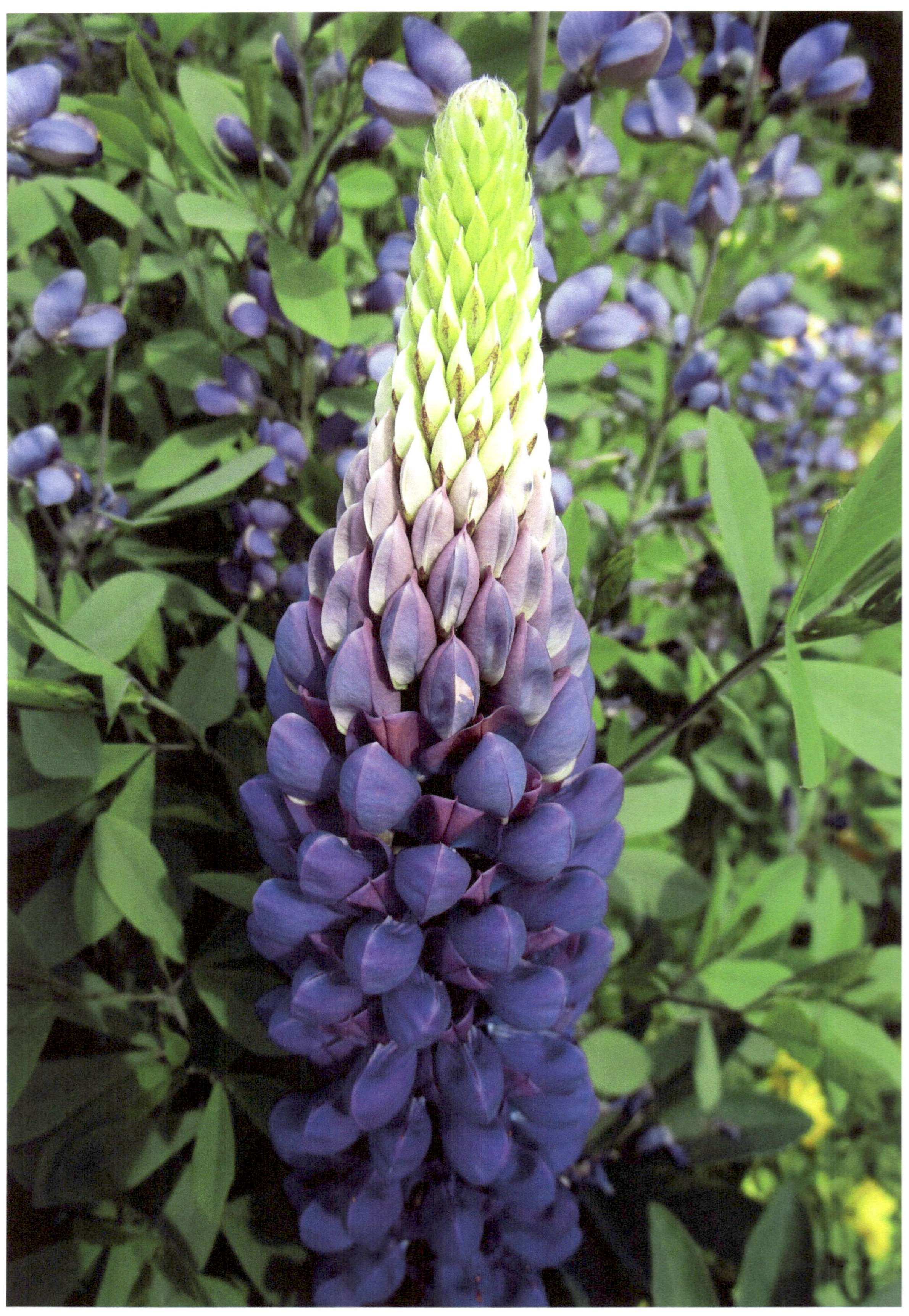

28. Marguerite Daisy (Argyranthemum frutescens)
    Colour: White; Yellow; Orange; Varied
    First Bloom: Late April to May
    Amount of Sun Needed: Wide Range from Mild to Full
    Scent: Minimal
    Petal Size: Small to Moderate

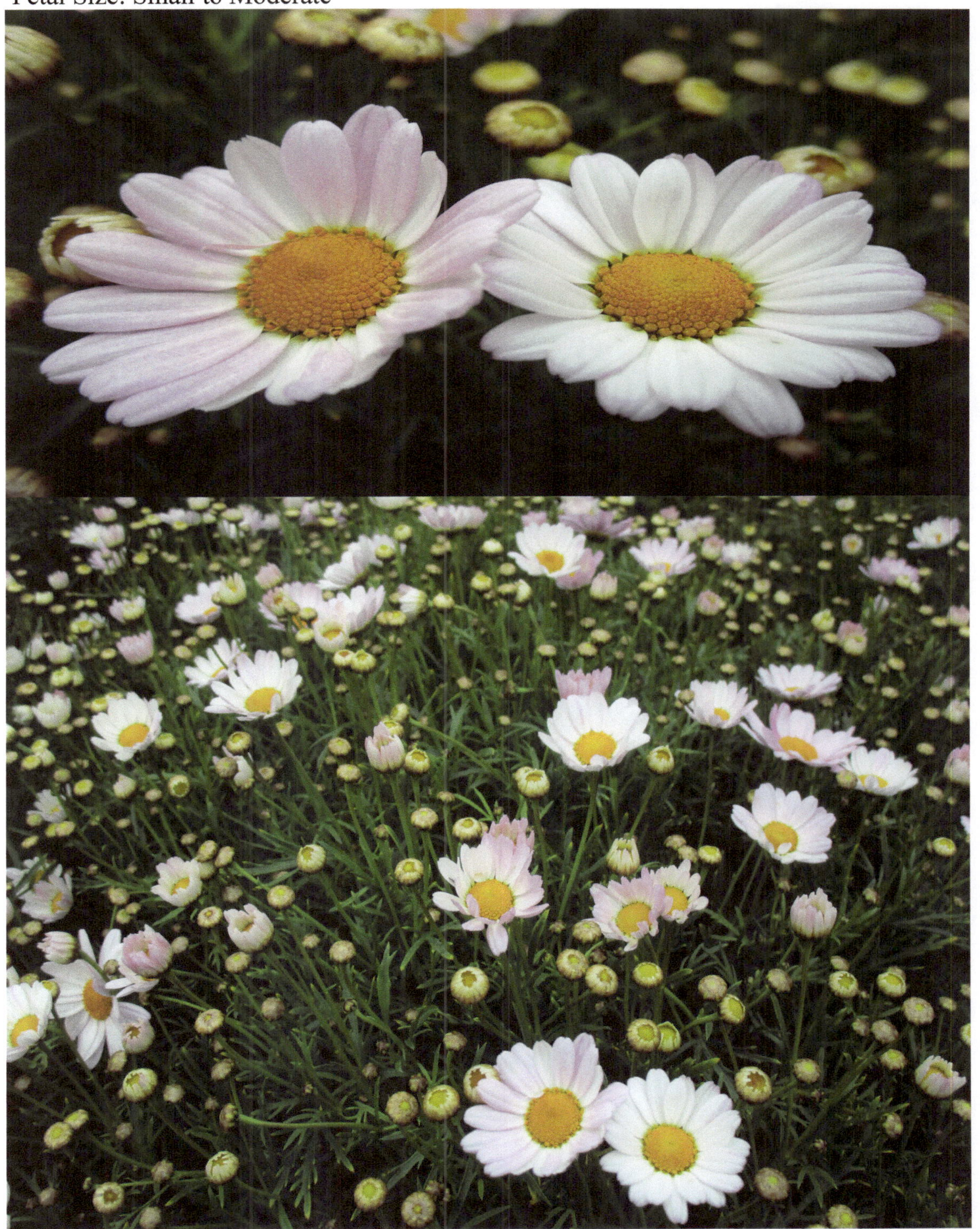

29. Nemesia (Nemesia caerulea)
    Colour: White; Light Pink; Light Blue; Purple; Yellow
    First Bloom: April
    Amount of Sun Needed: Moderate
    Scent: None
    Petal Size: Medium

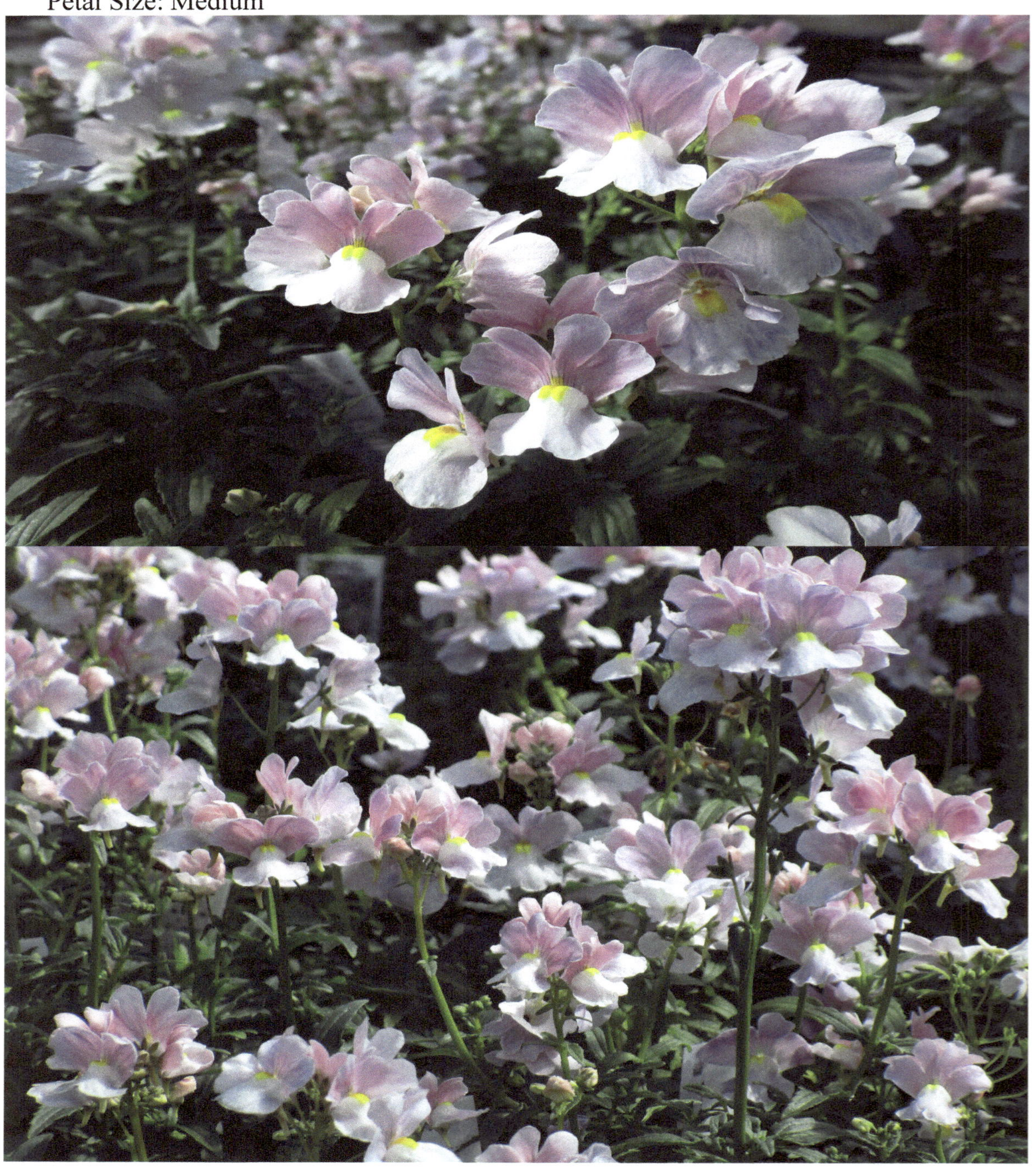

30. Pansy (Viola tricolor var. hortensis)
    Colour: Purple; Blue; Yellow; Orange; White; Varied
    First Bloom: March
    Amount of Sun Needed: Moderate
    Scent: None
    Petal Size: Small to Medium

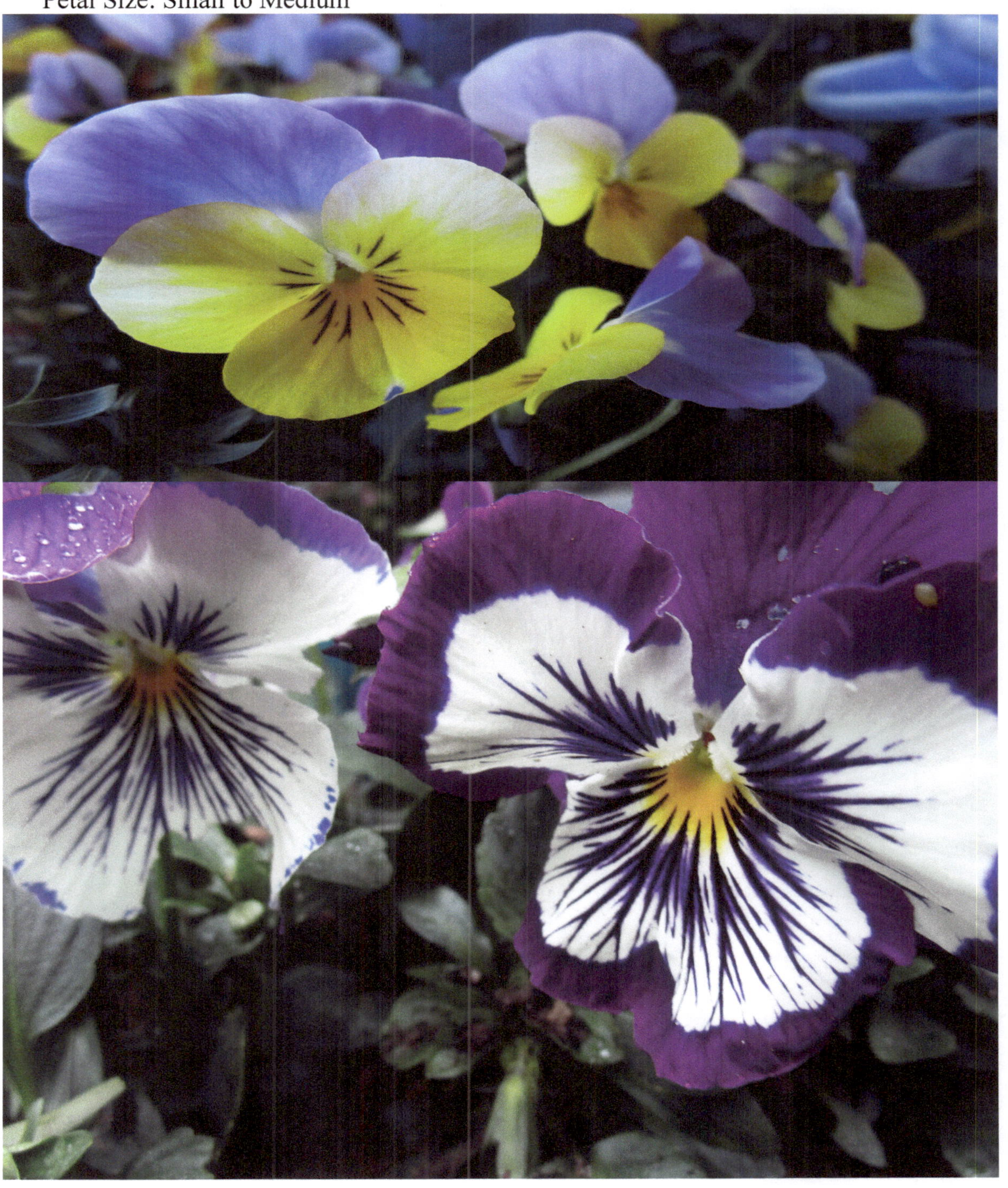

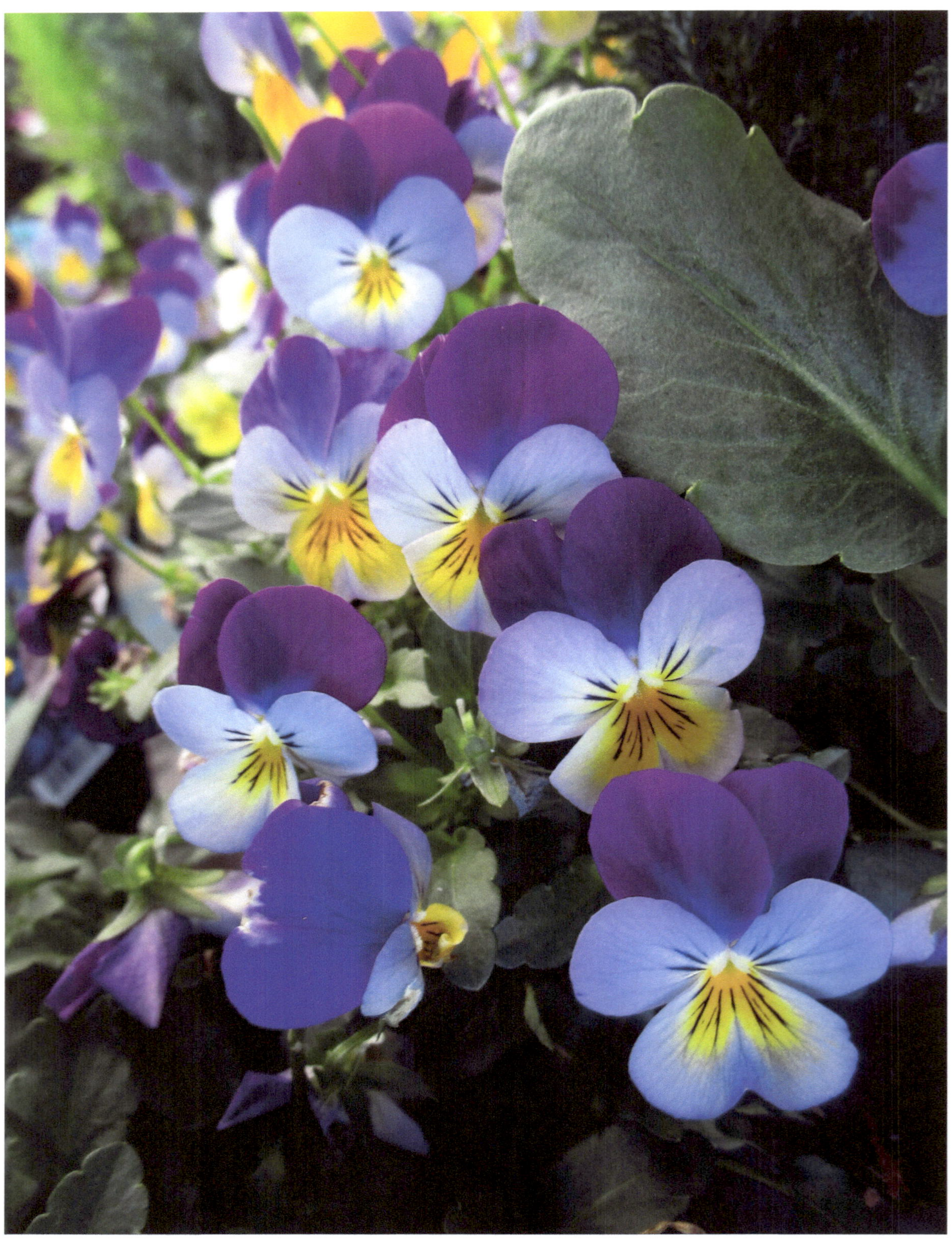

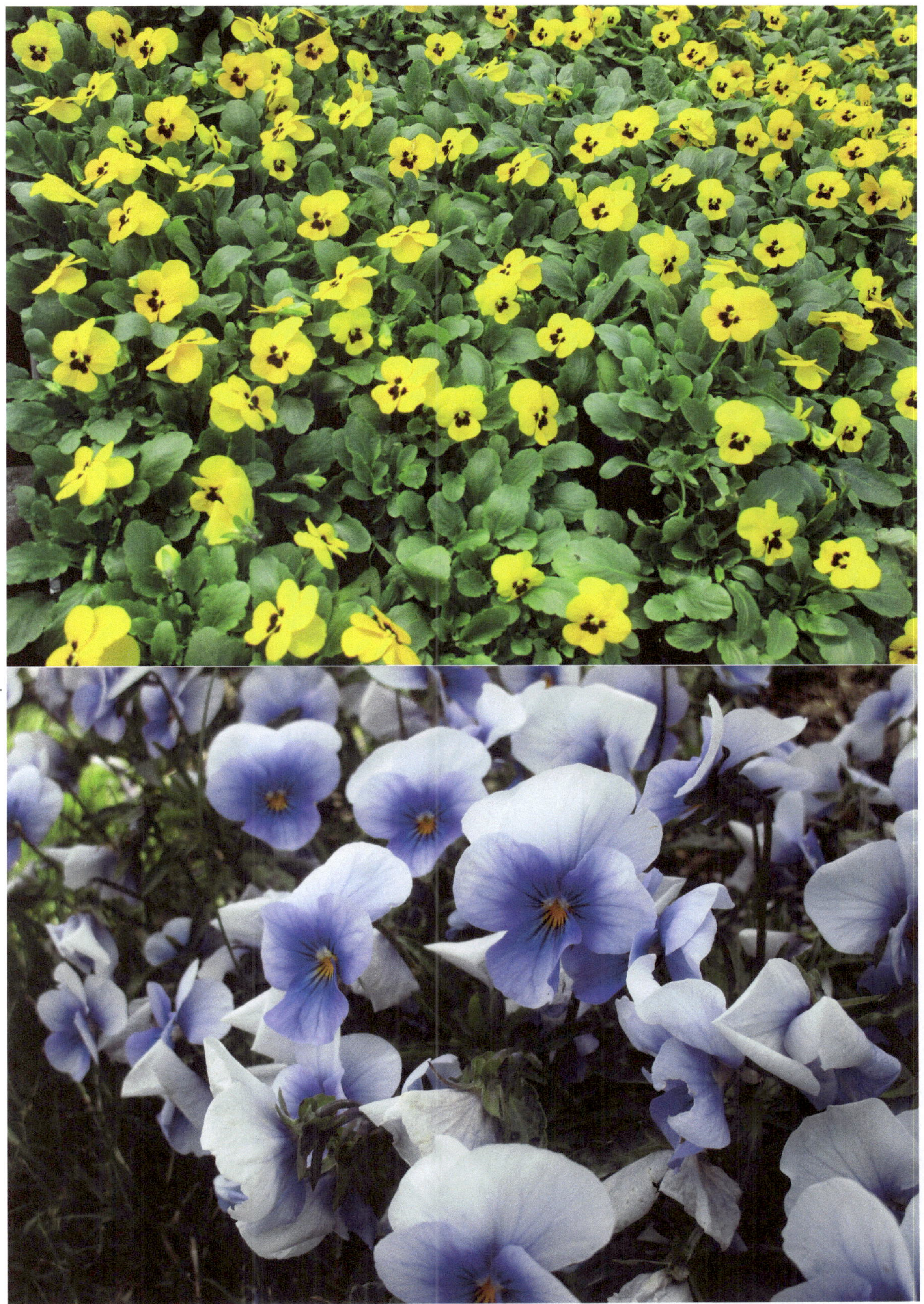

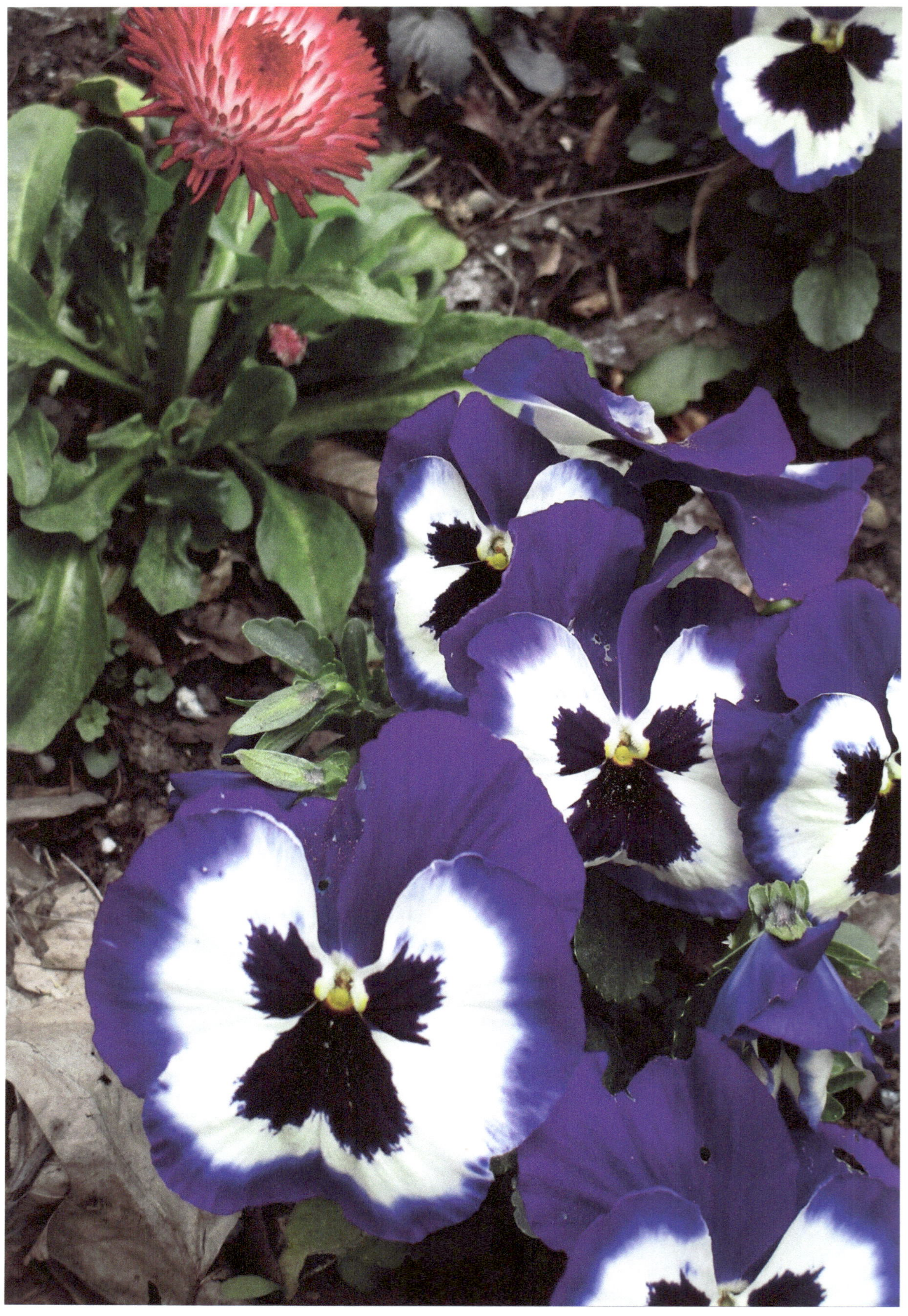

31. Petunia (Petunia)
   Colour: Purple; Blue; Yellow; Pink; Varied
   First Bloom: April
   Amount of Sun Needed: Moderate to Full
   Scent: None
   Petal Size: Small to Medium

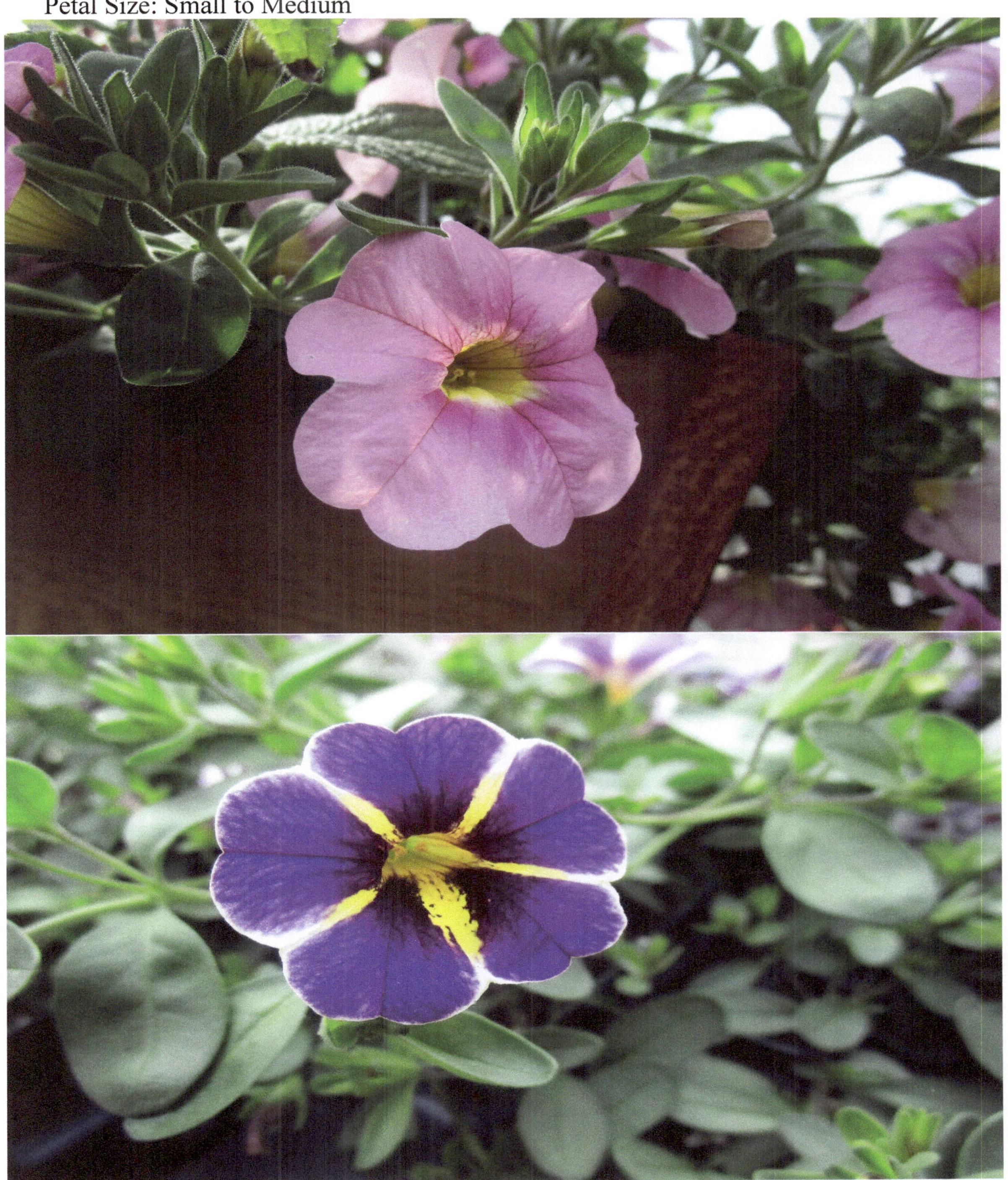

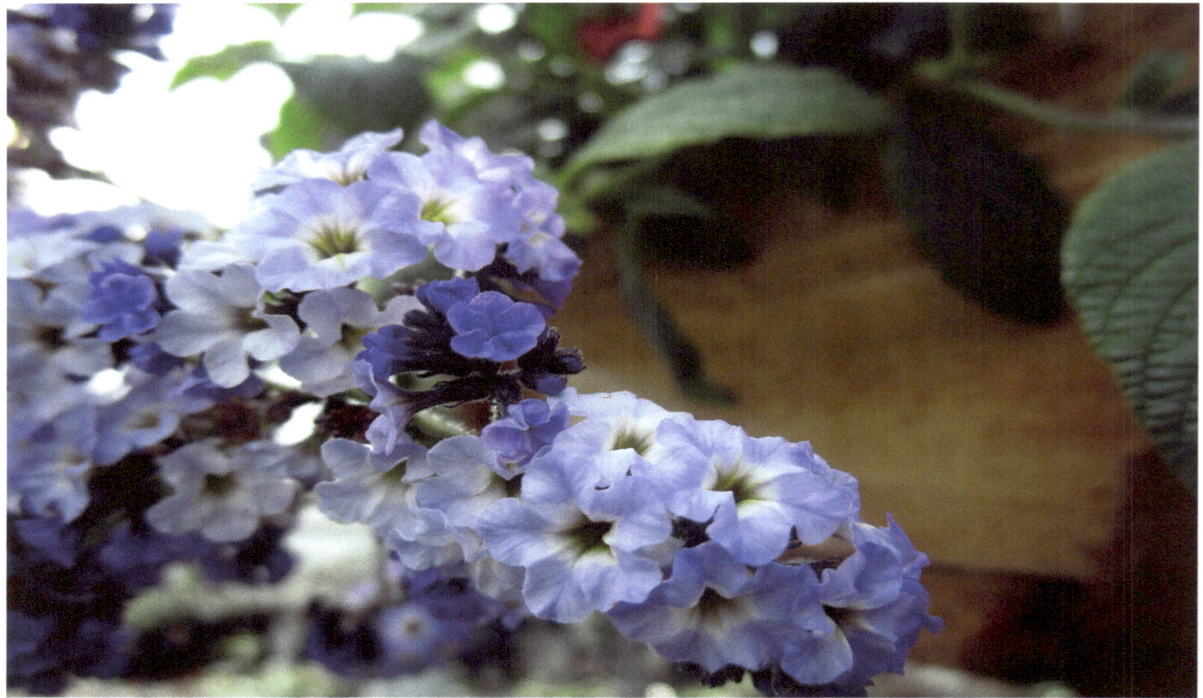

With dangling flower stalks and bright petals, petunias are often the foremost choice for hanging baskets.

32. Plum Blossom (Prunus Mume)
    Colour: Red, Pink, White, Yellow(Stamen)
    First Bloom: March
    Amount of Sun Needed: Moderate to Full
    Scent: Mild to Strong
    Petal Size: Small to Medium

"Cherry Plum Blossom"

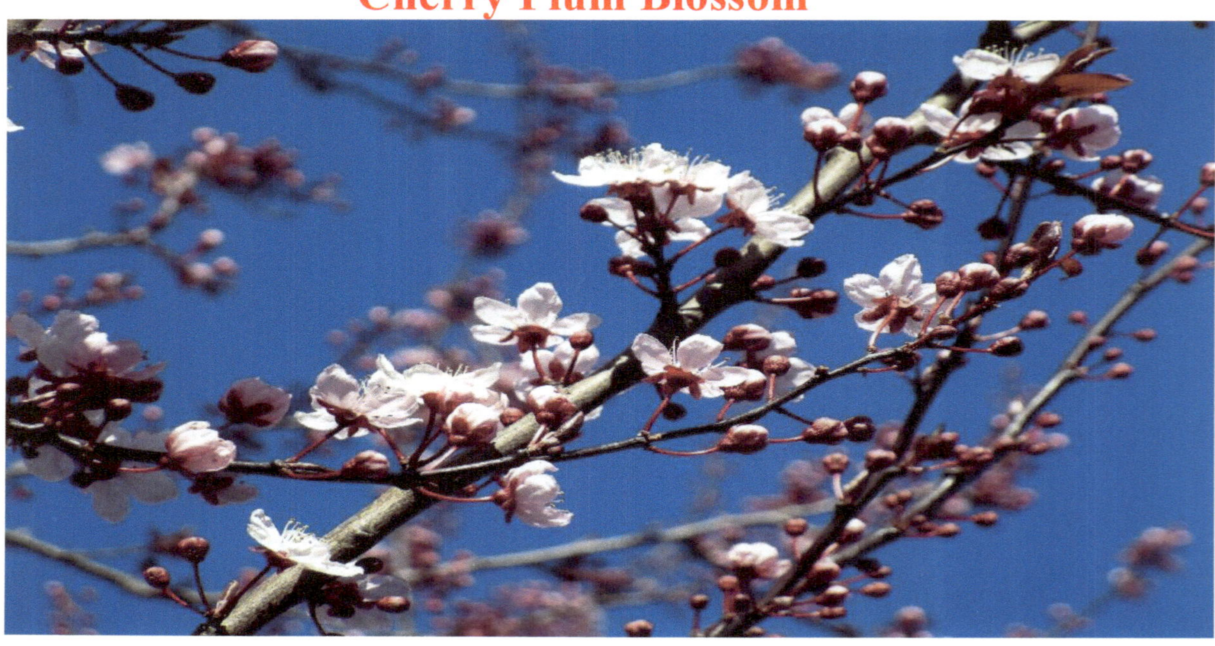

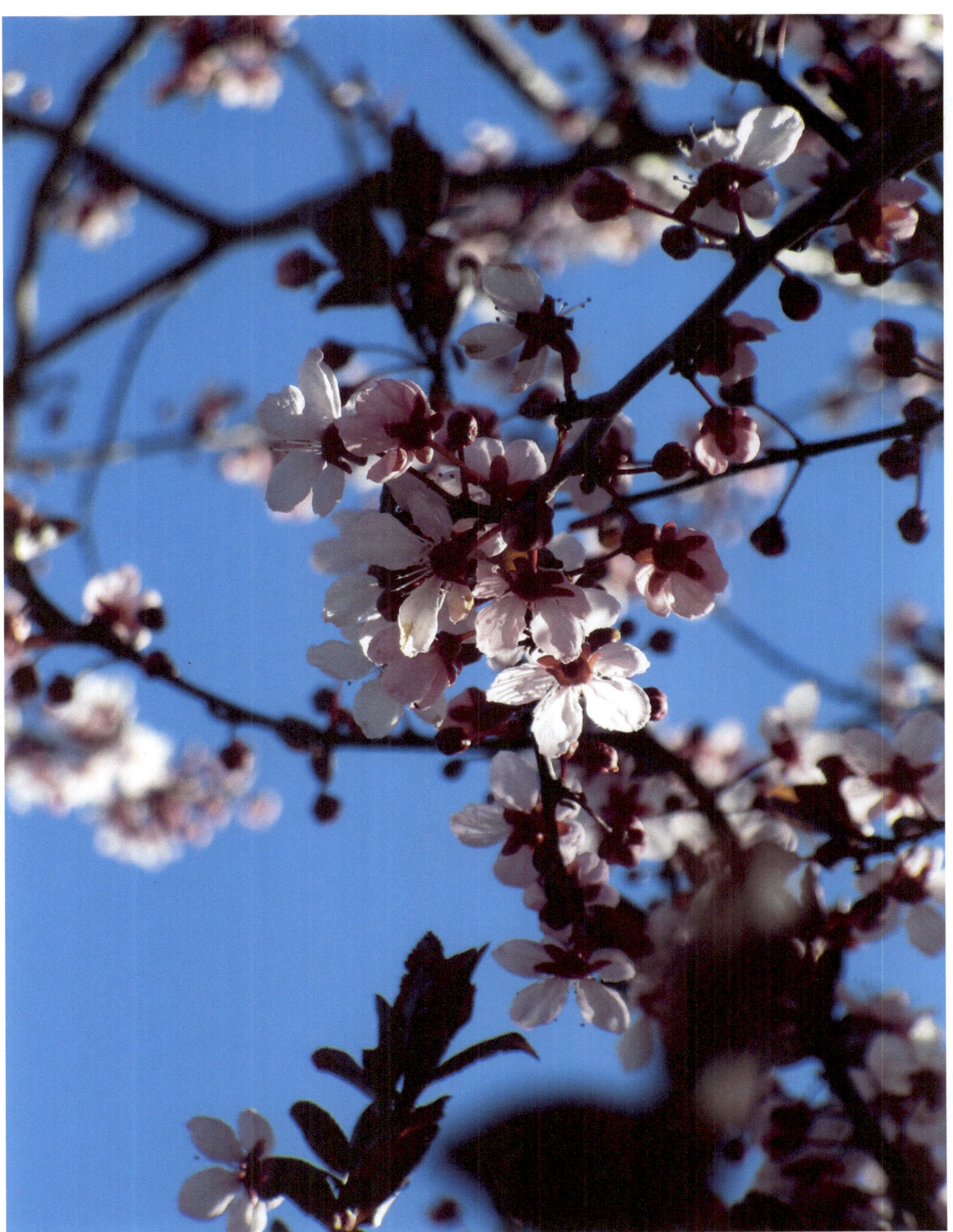

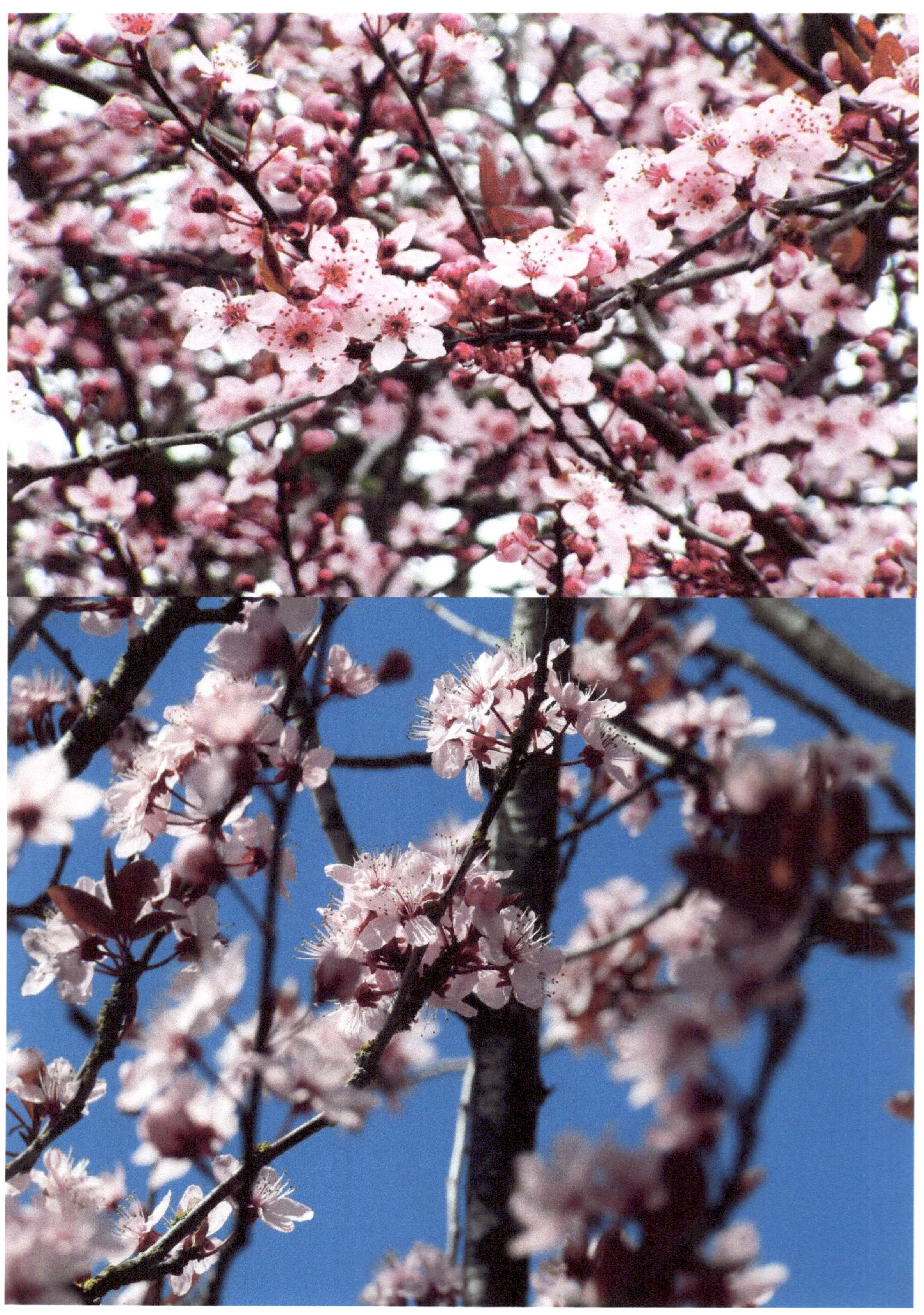

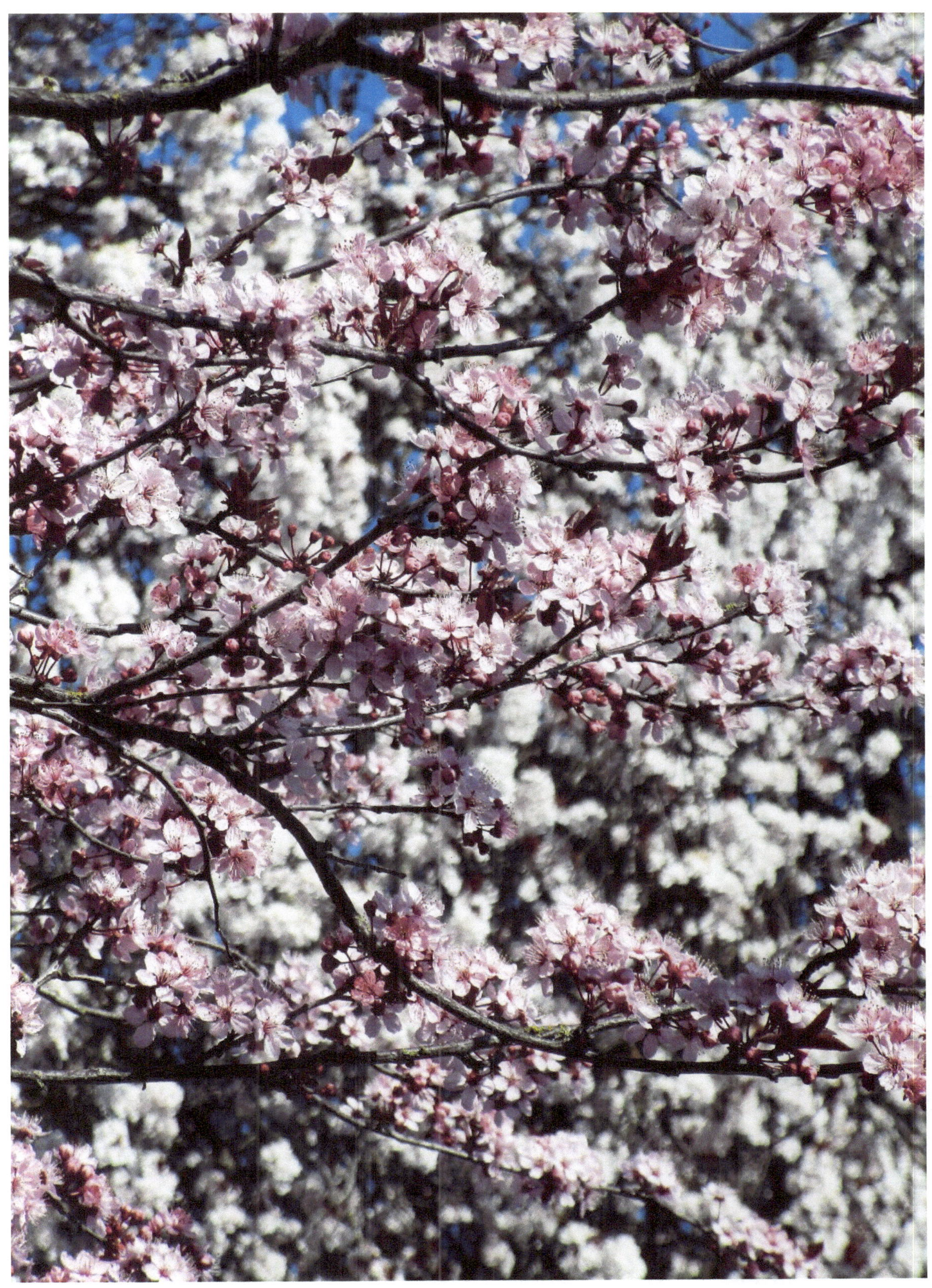

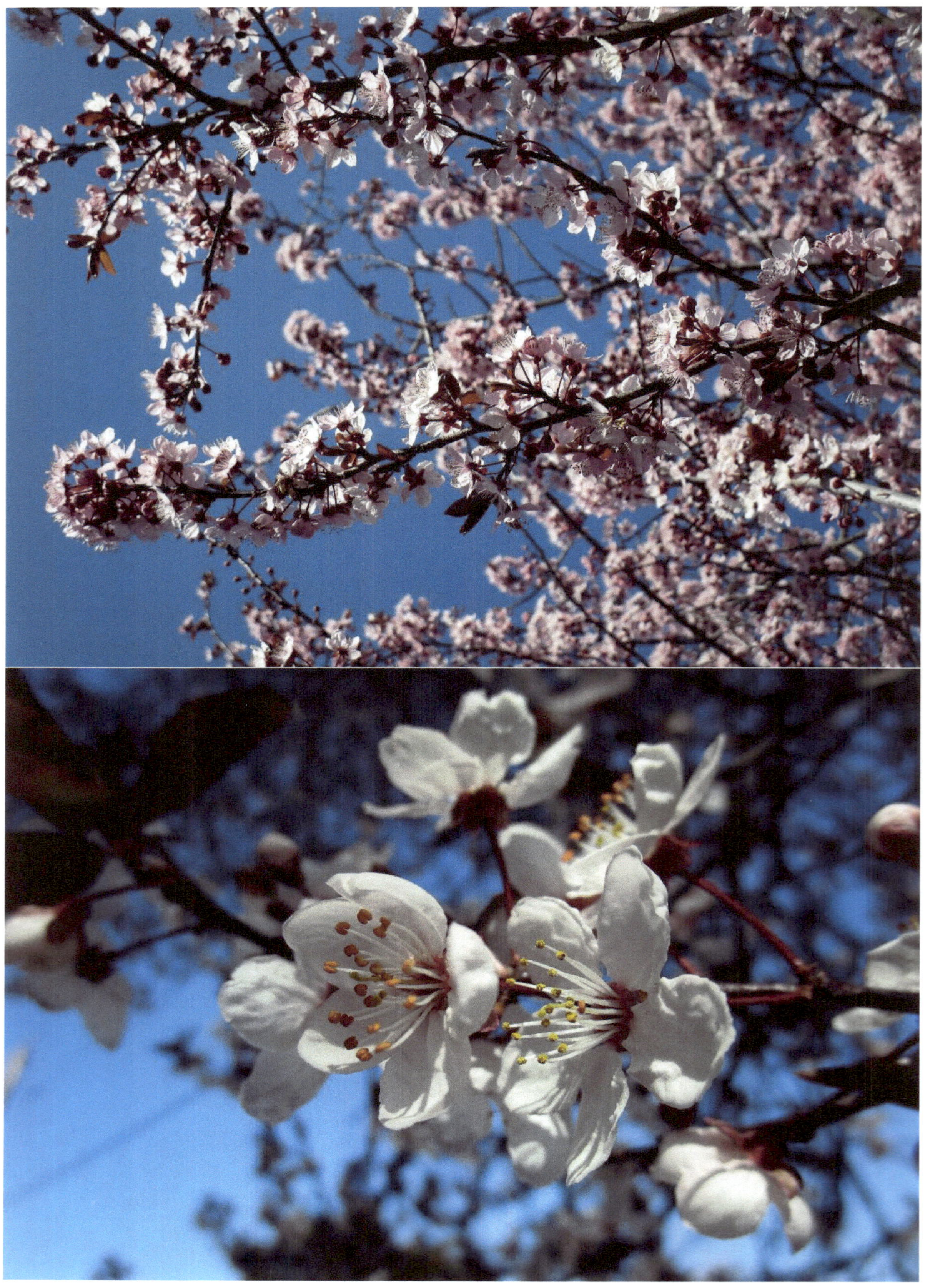

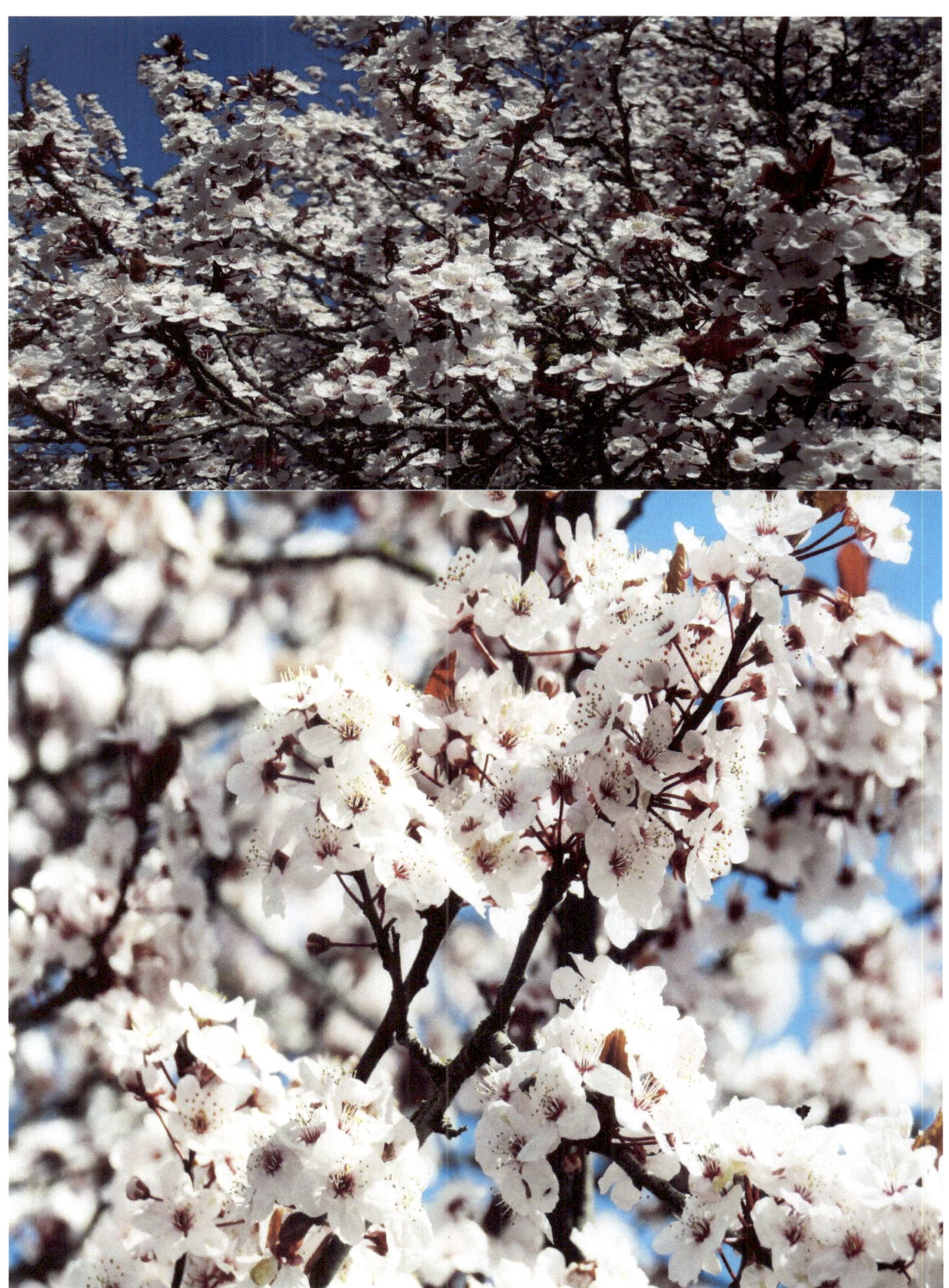

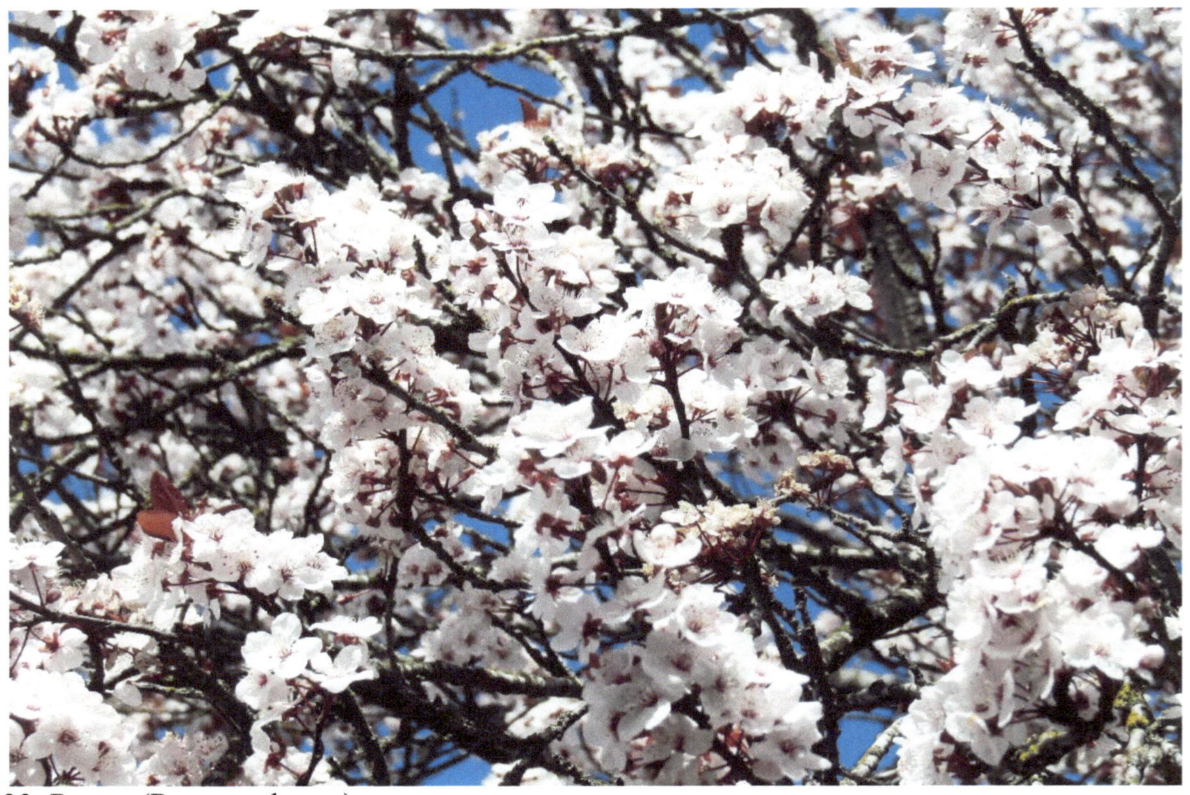

33. Poppy (Papaver rhoeas)
    Colour: Red, Pink, Black(centre)
    First Bloom: June
    Amount of Sun Needed: Moderate to Full
    Scent: None
    Petal Size: Fairly Large

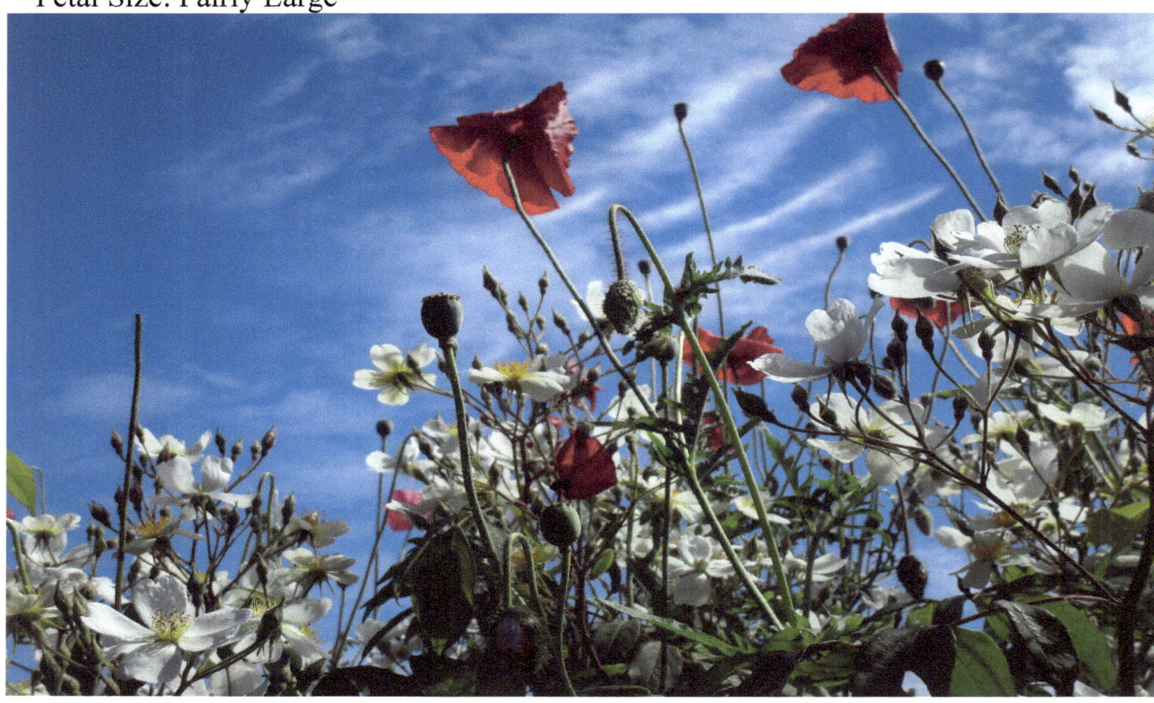

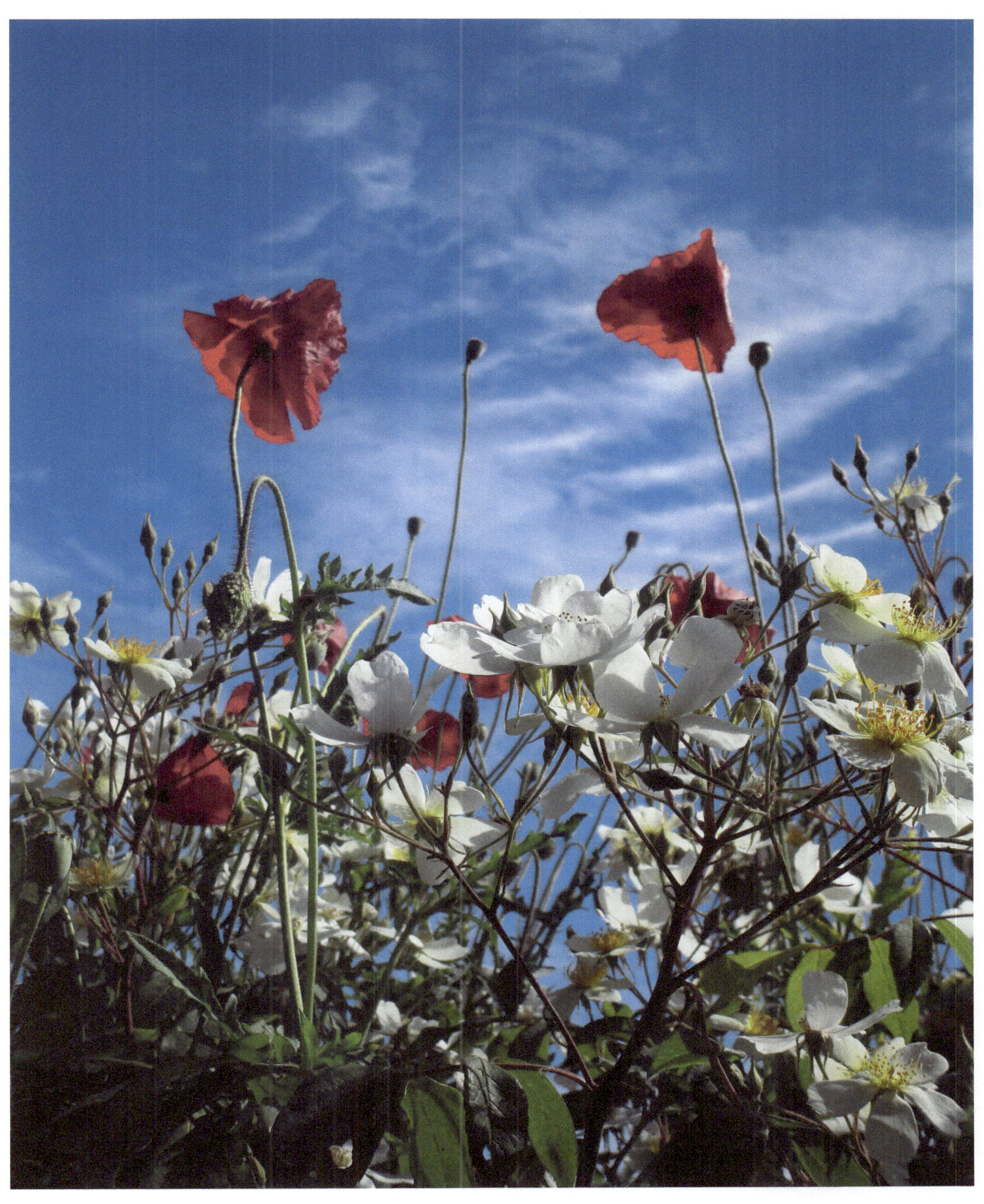

A long-time symbol for veterans' Remembrance Day, red poppy flowers serve as a nice colour complement to other flower mix in public park gardens such as the Queen Elizabeth Rose Garden, as in the above.

34. "Pretty Lady" Rose by Floribunda(Rosa)
Colour: Peach;Pink;White
First Bloom: June
Amount of Sun Needed:Mild to Moderate
Scent: None
Petal Size: Medium

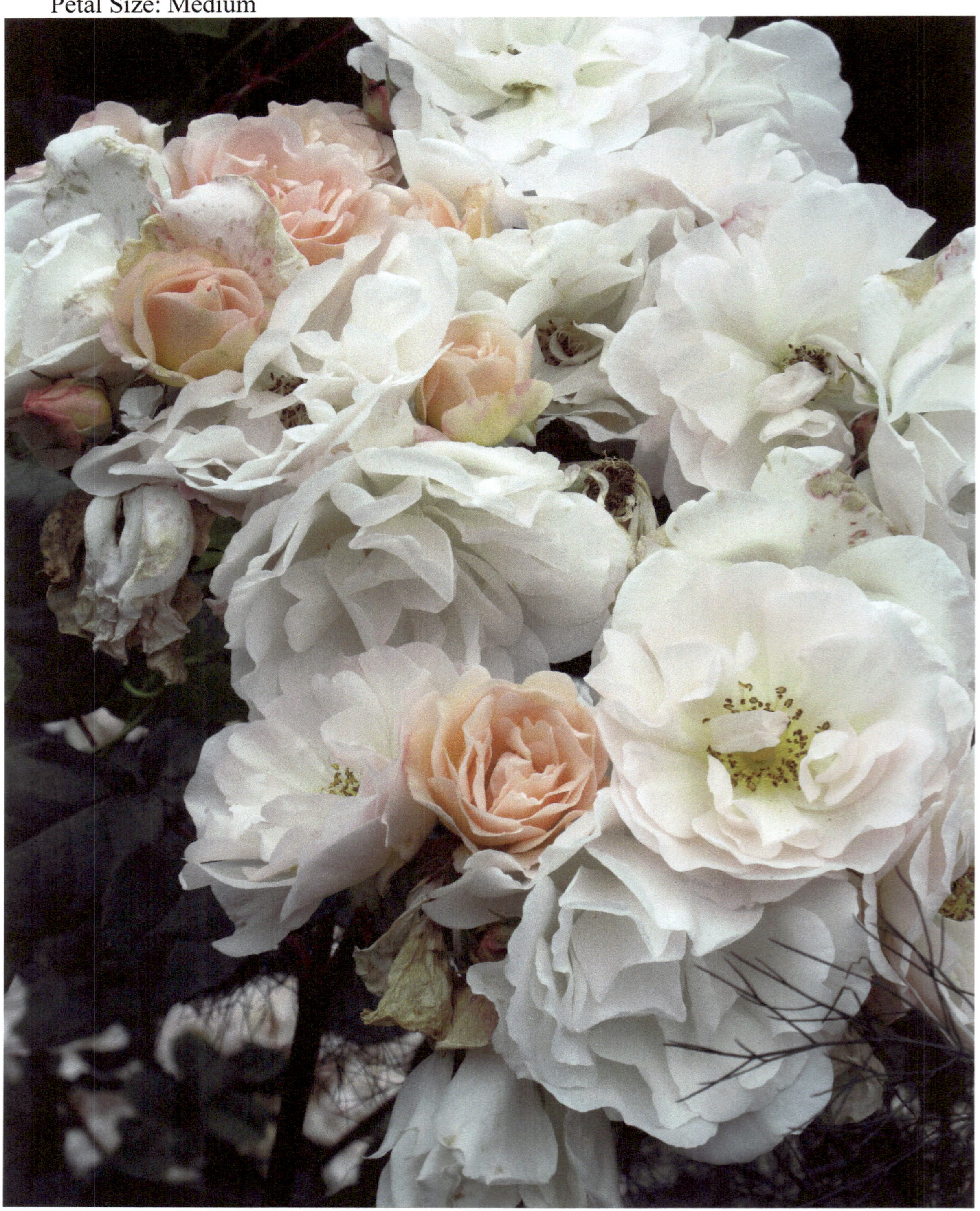

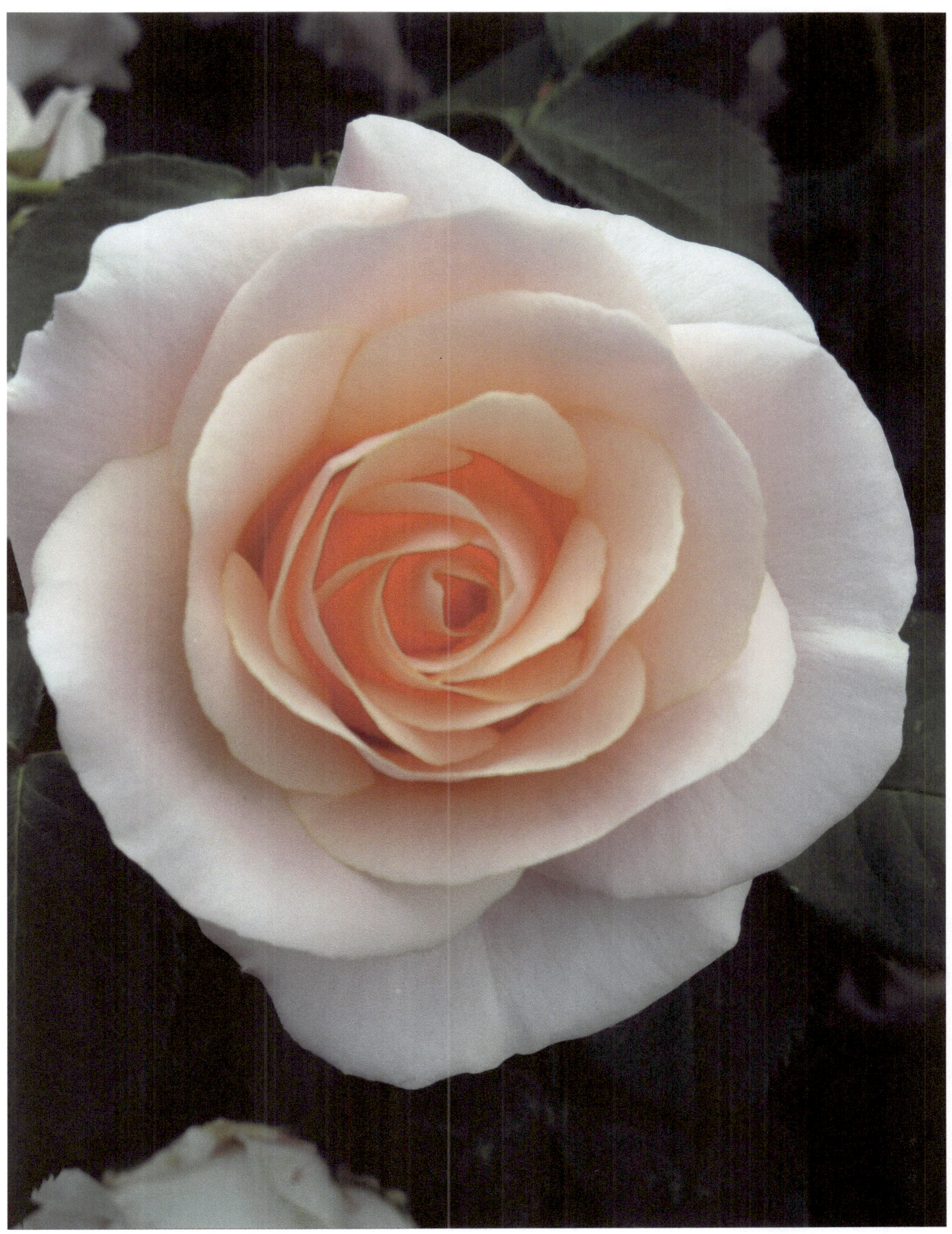

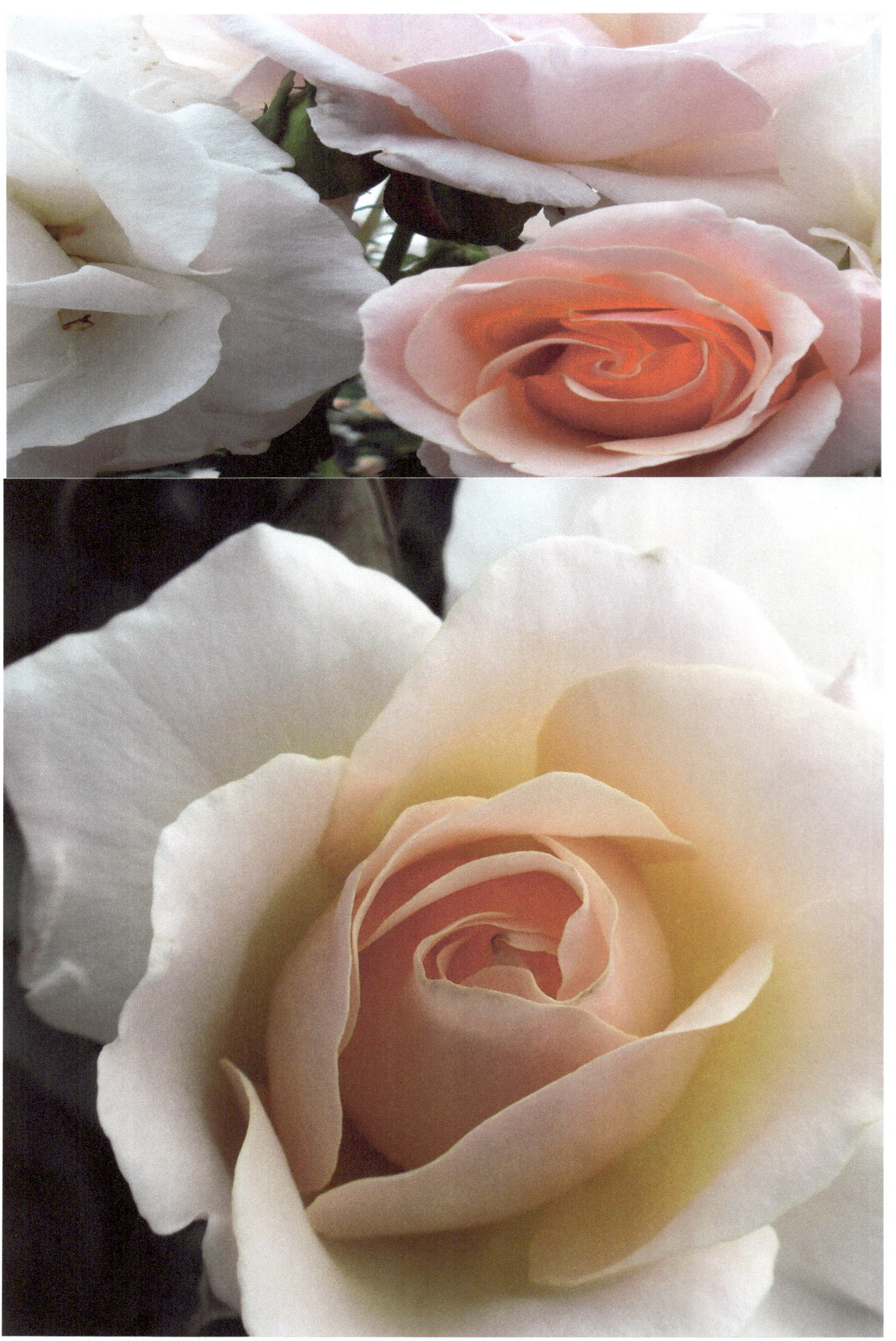

35. Primrose (Primula vulgaris)
   Colour: Blue; Purple; Yellow; Pink; Red; Orange; White; Varied
   First Bloom: Late February
   Amount of Sun Needed: Mild to Moderate
   Scent: None
   Petal Size: Medium

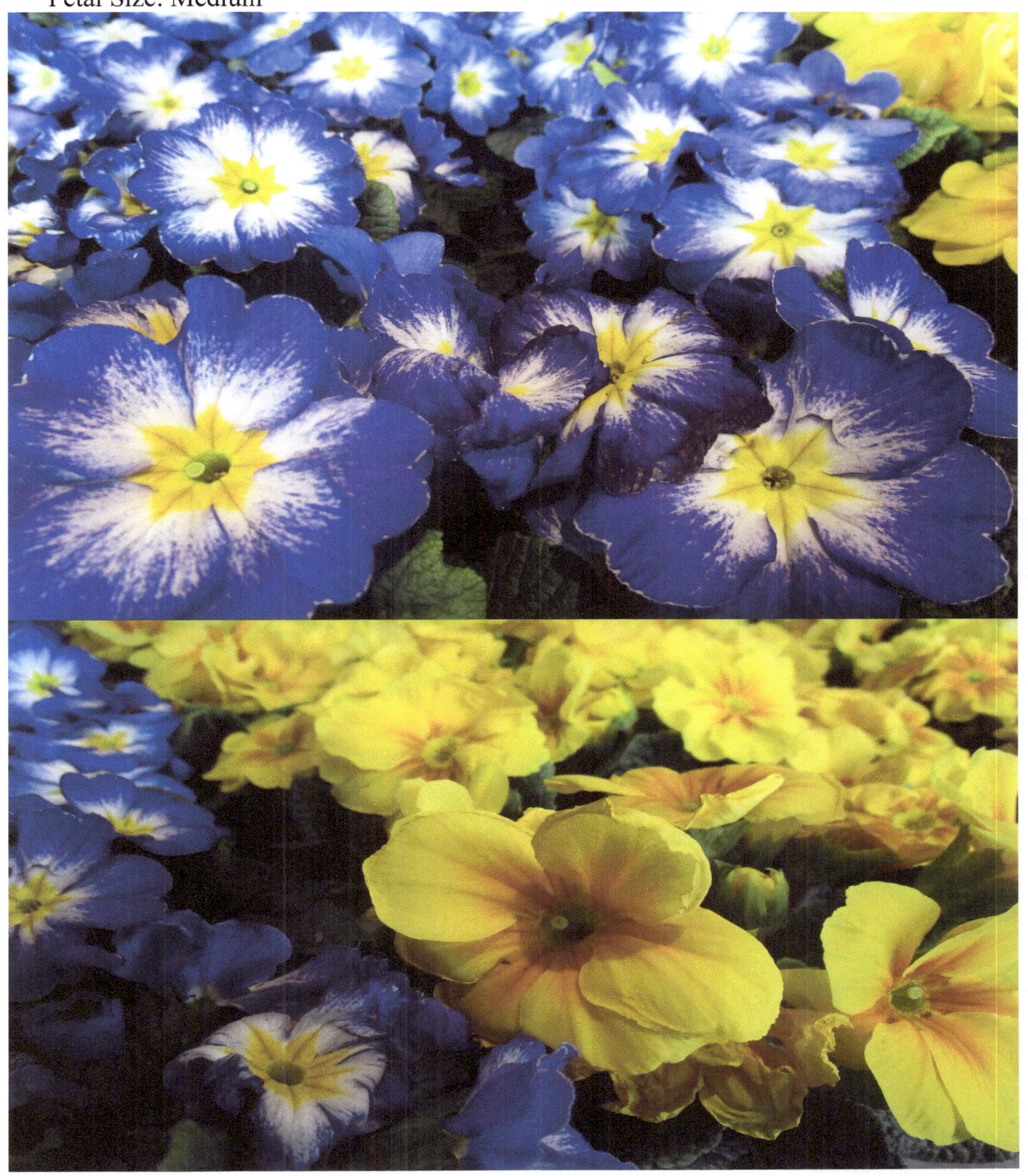

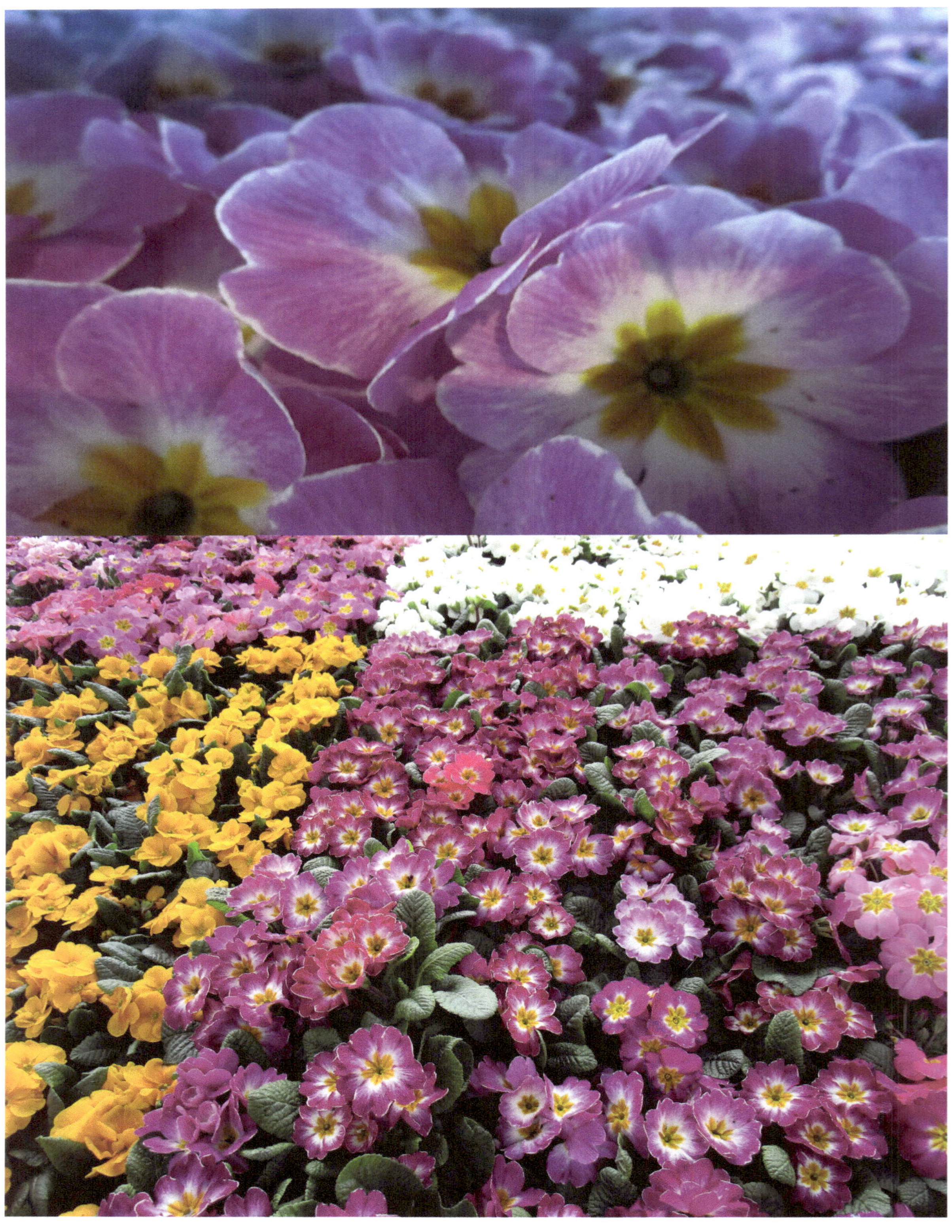

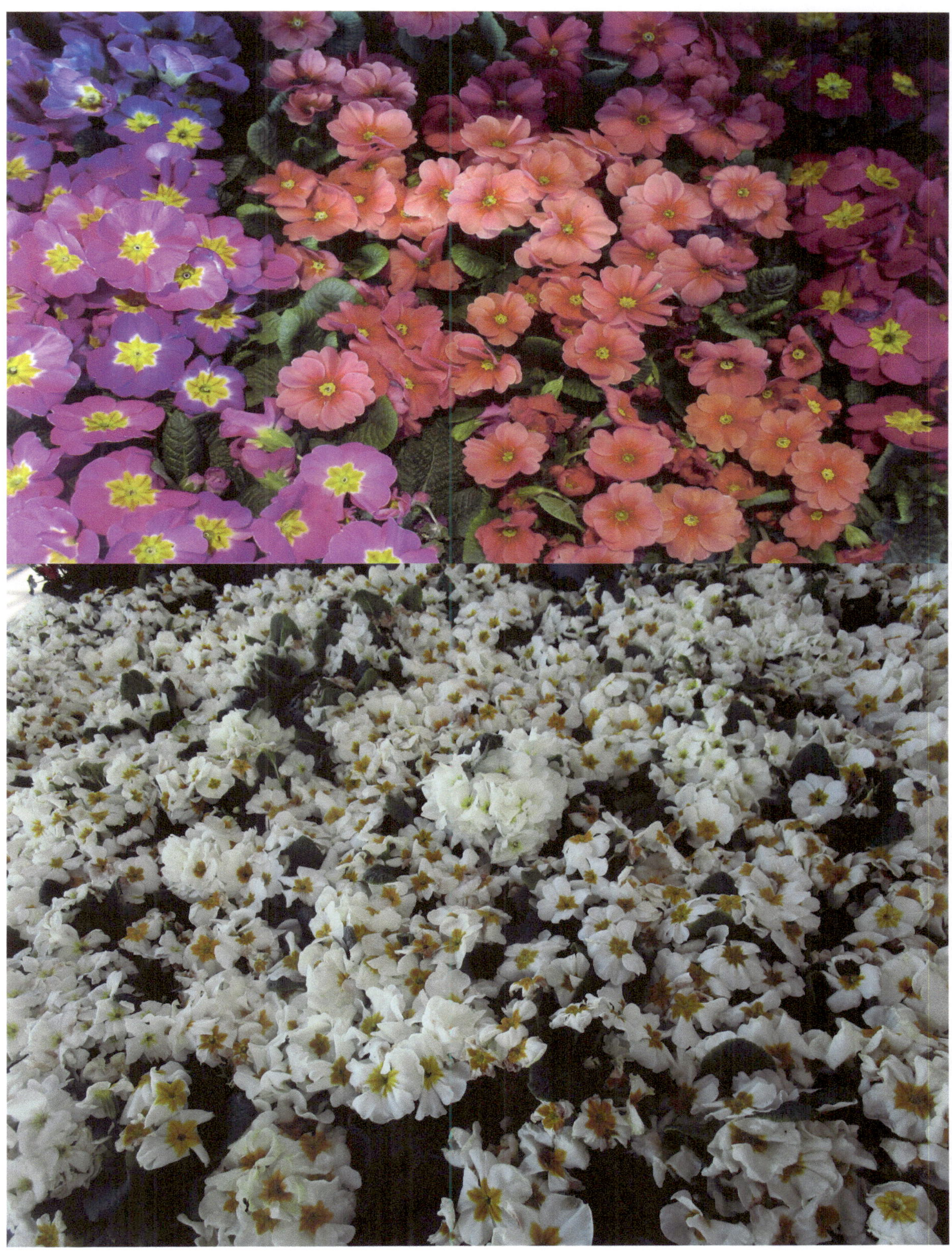

The first bloom of a colorful variety of Primrose in late February heralded the start of the 2019 flowering season in Vancouver as garden centres and shops began filling their shelves and display areas with these early blossoms of the year.

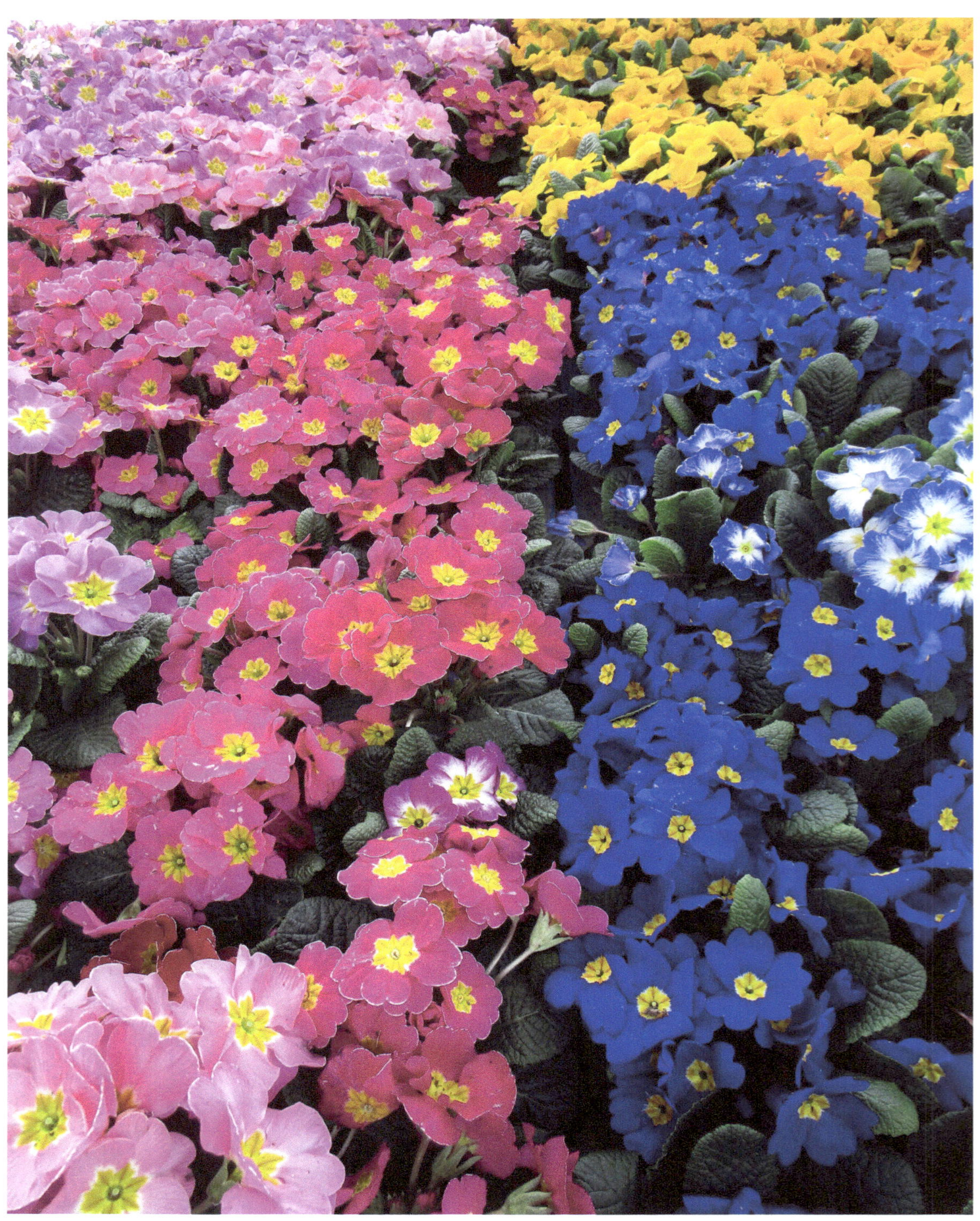

36. "Rhapsody in Blue" Rose(Rosa)
    Colour: Purple; Violet; Yellow(Stamen)
    First Bloom: August
    Amount of Sun Needed: Moderate to Full
    Scent: None
    Petal Size: Medium

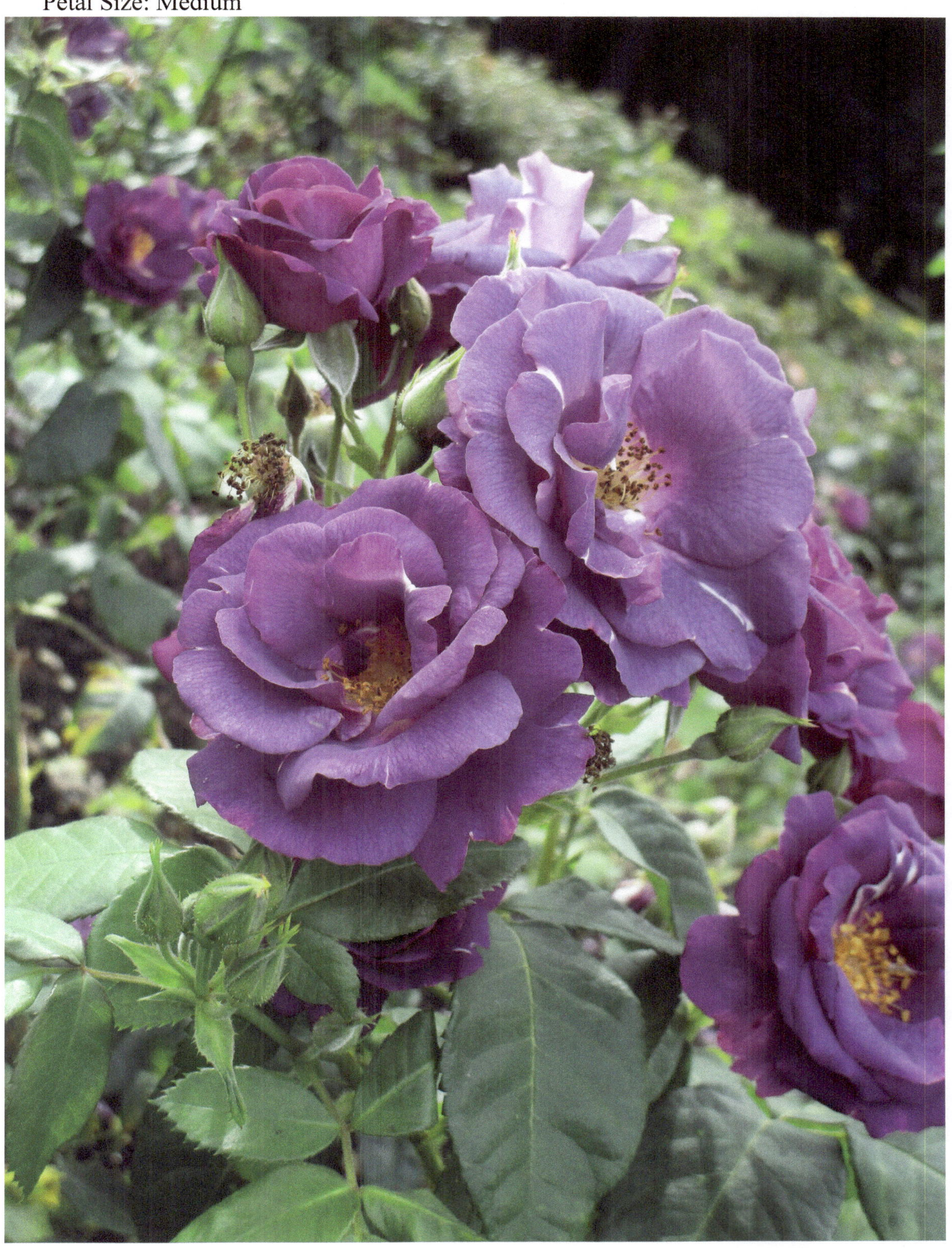

37. Romantica Hybrid Tea Rose (Rosa 'Frederic Mistral')
Colour: Shell Pink
First Bloom: September
Amount of Sun Needed: Mild to Moderate
Scent: None
Petal Size: Medium

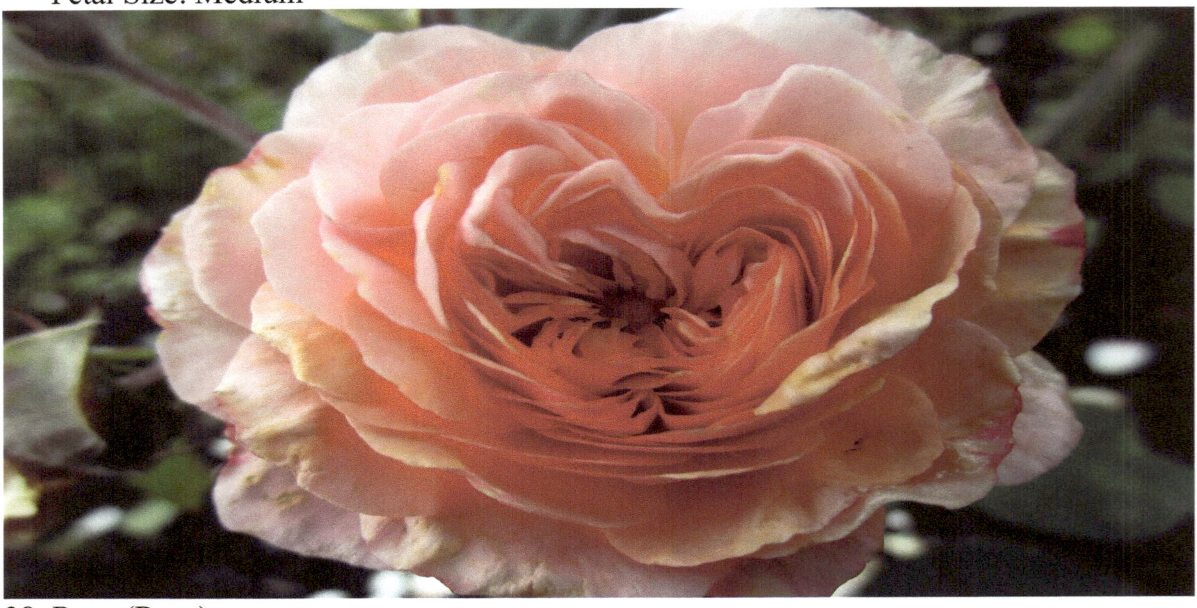

38. Rose (Rosa)
Colour: Varied
First Bloom: Late Spring May to June
Amount of Sun Needed: Moderate to Full
Scent: Varied
Petal Size: Varied

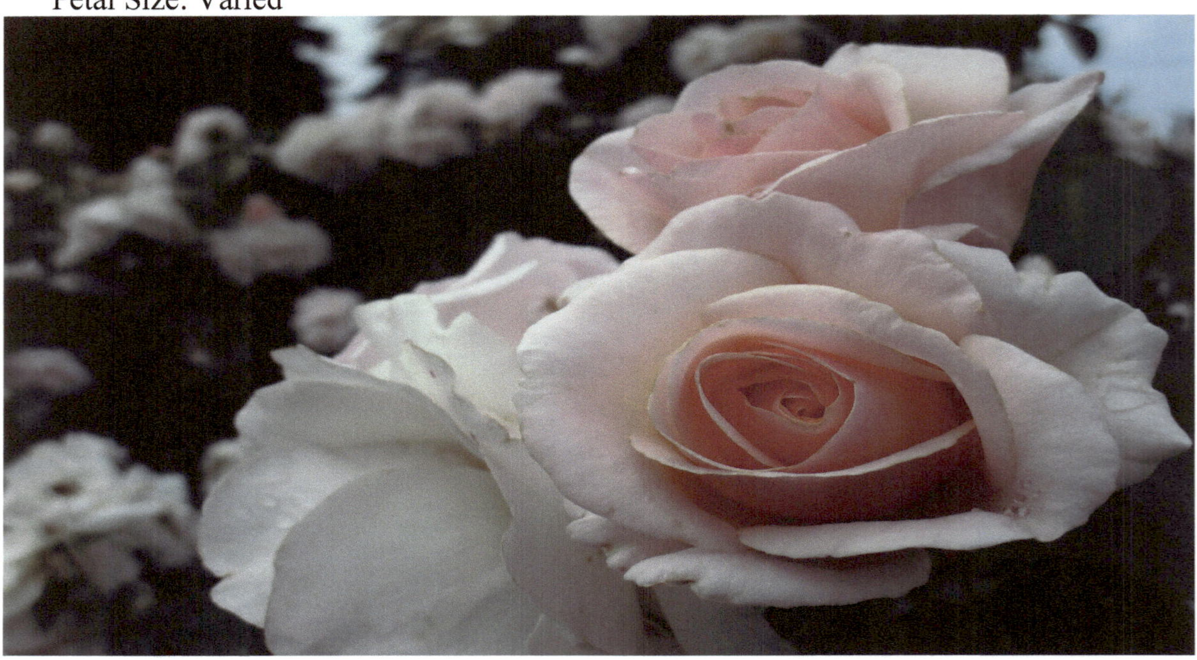

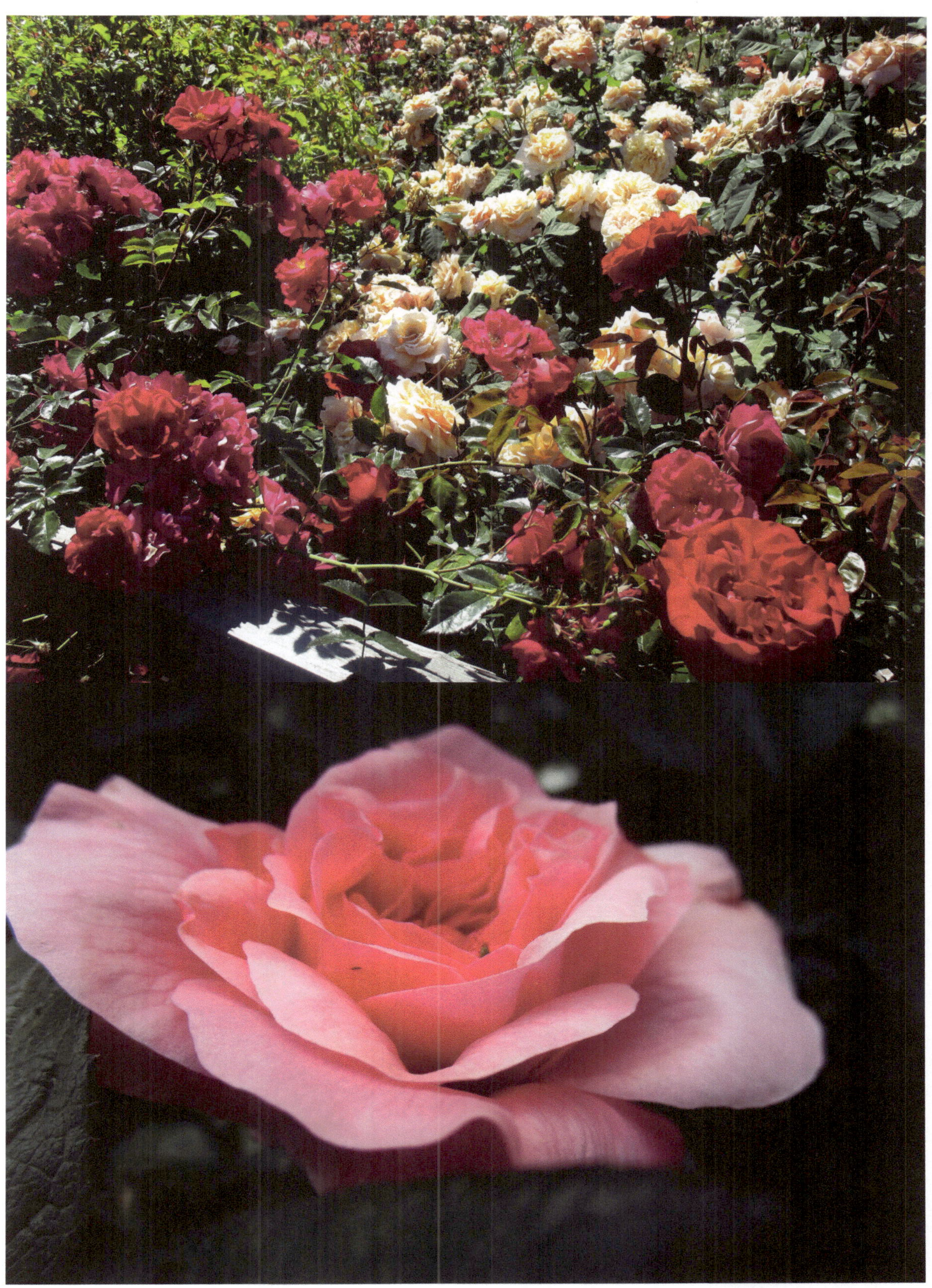

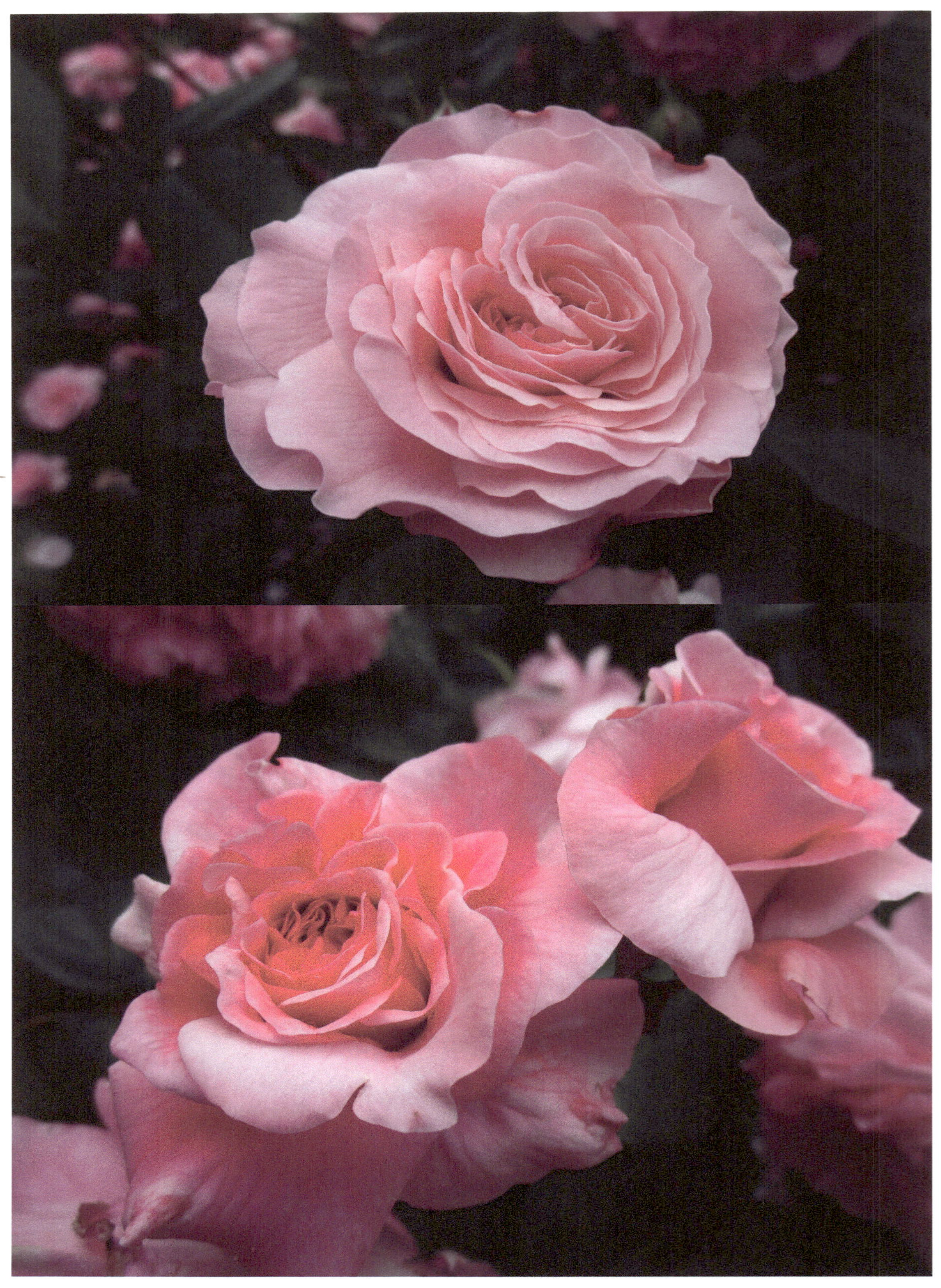

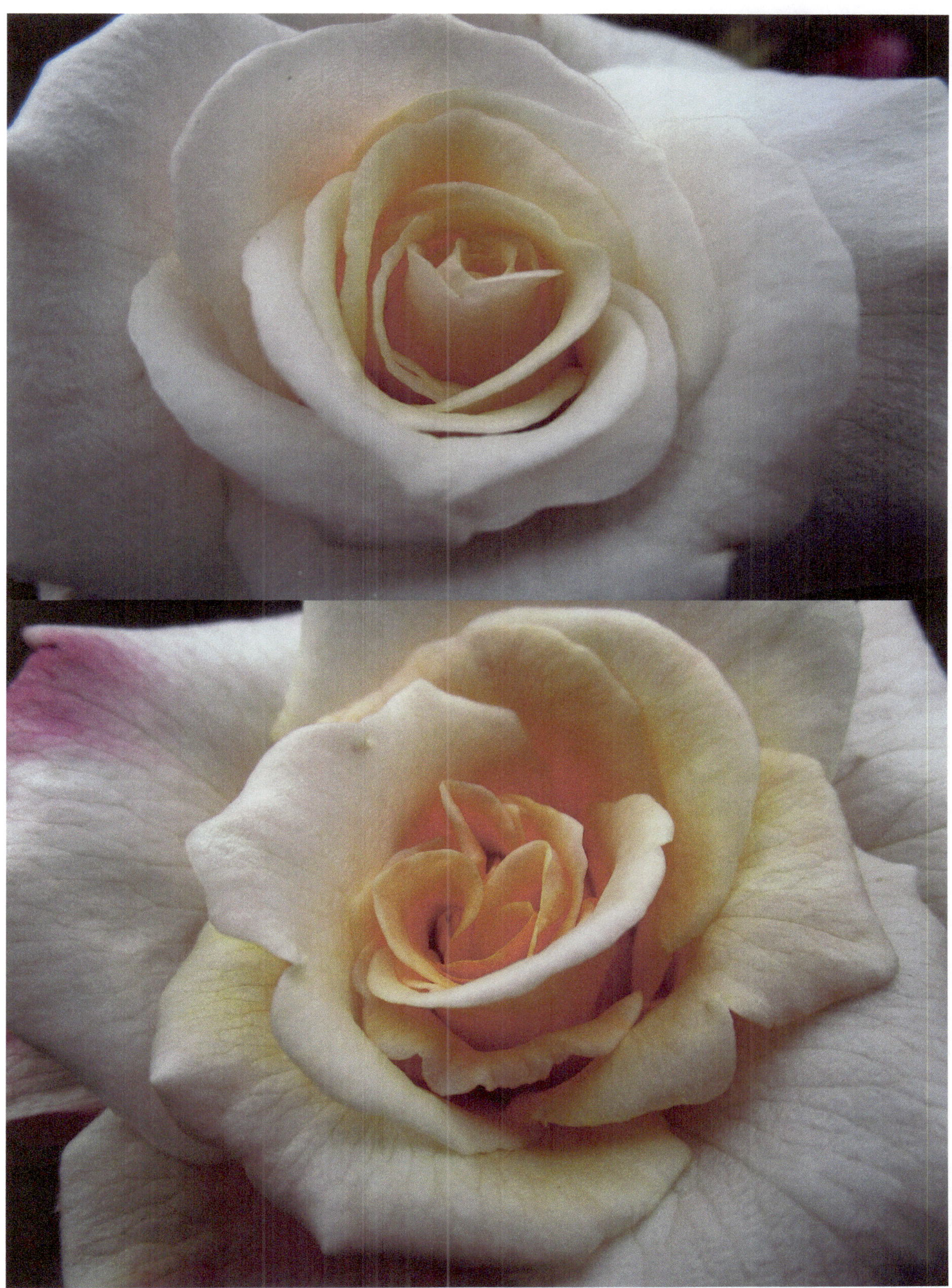

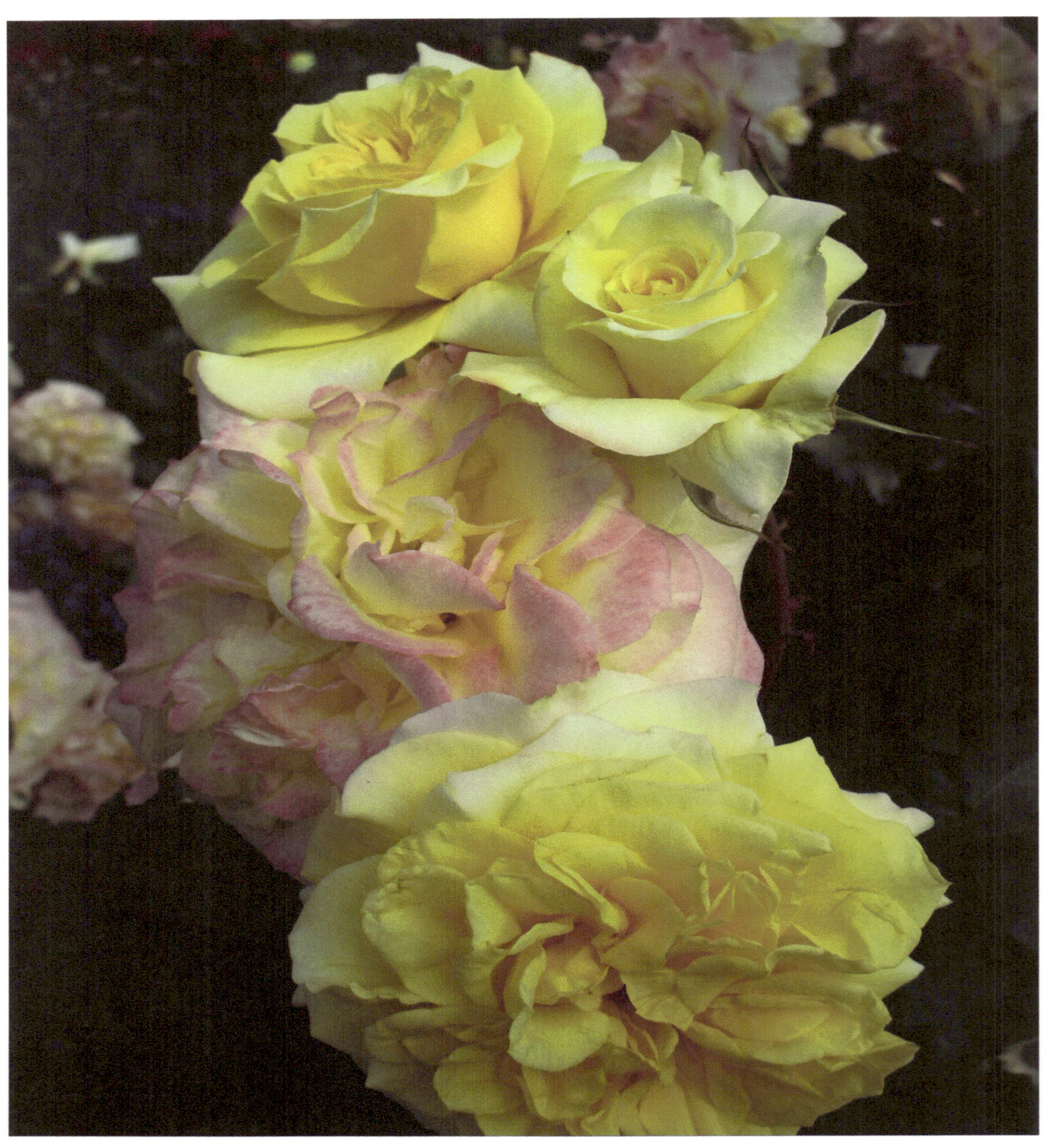

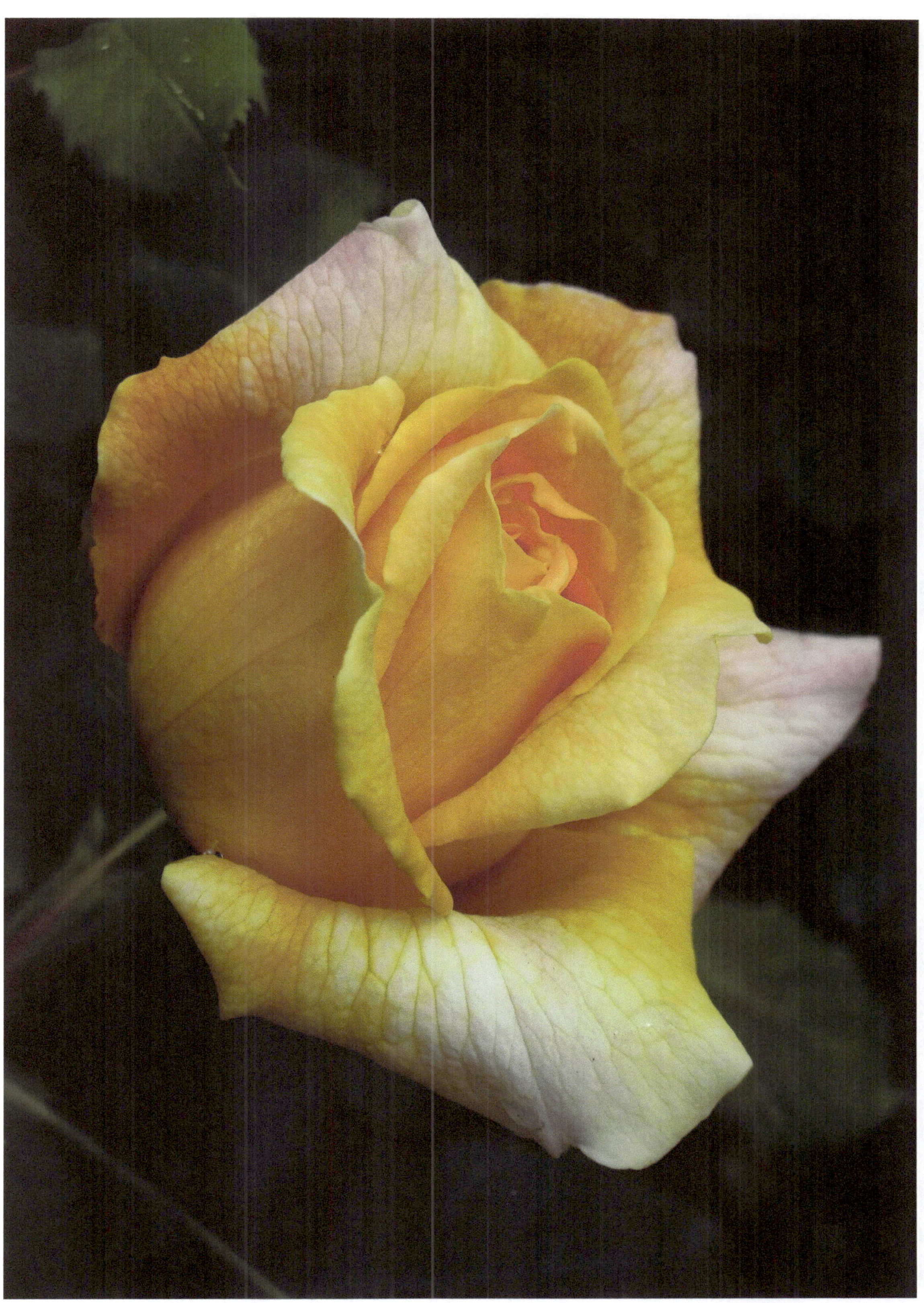

39. Royal Candle (Veronica spicata)
   Colour: Red
   First Bloom: May
   Amount of Sun Needed: Mild to Moderate
   Scent: None
   Petal Size: Small

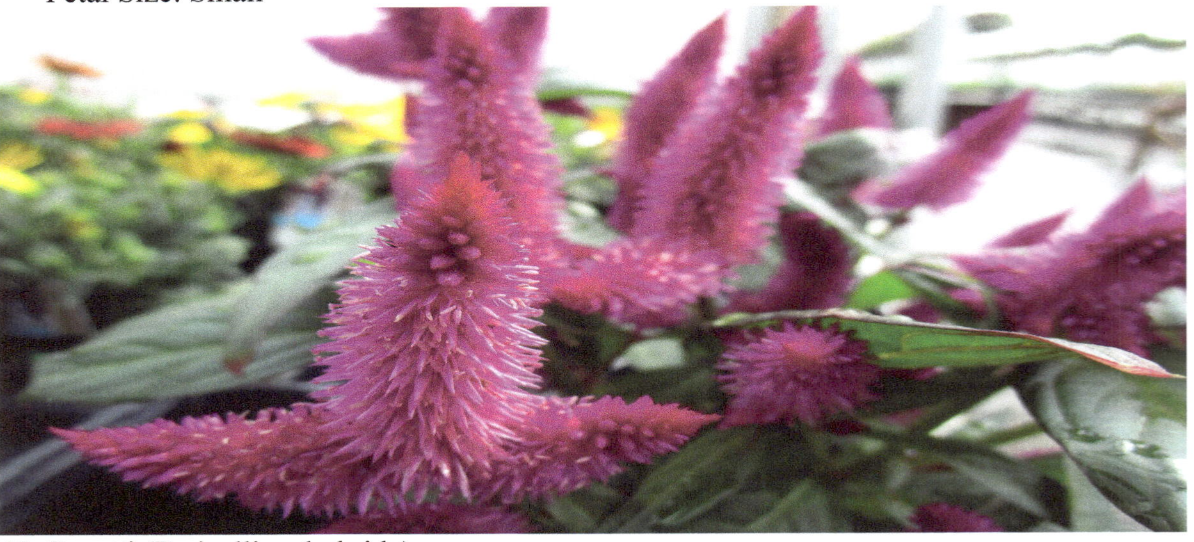

40. Senetti (Pericallis x hybrida)
   Colour: White; Light Purple; Blue; Pink; Yellow; Varied
   First Bloom: May
   Amount of Sun Needed: Moderate to Full
   Scent: None
   Petal Size: Medium

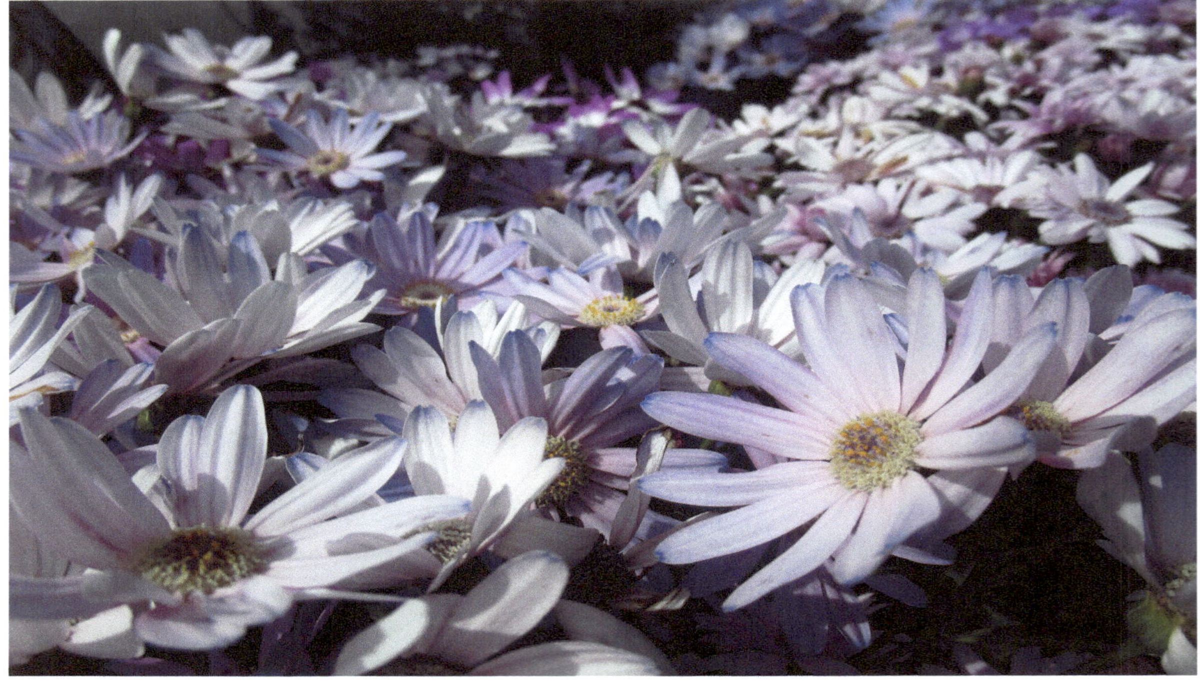

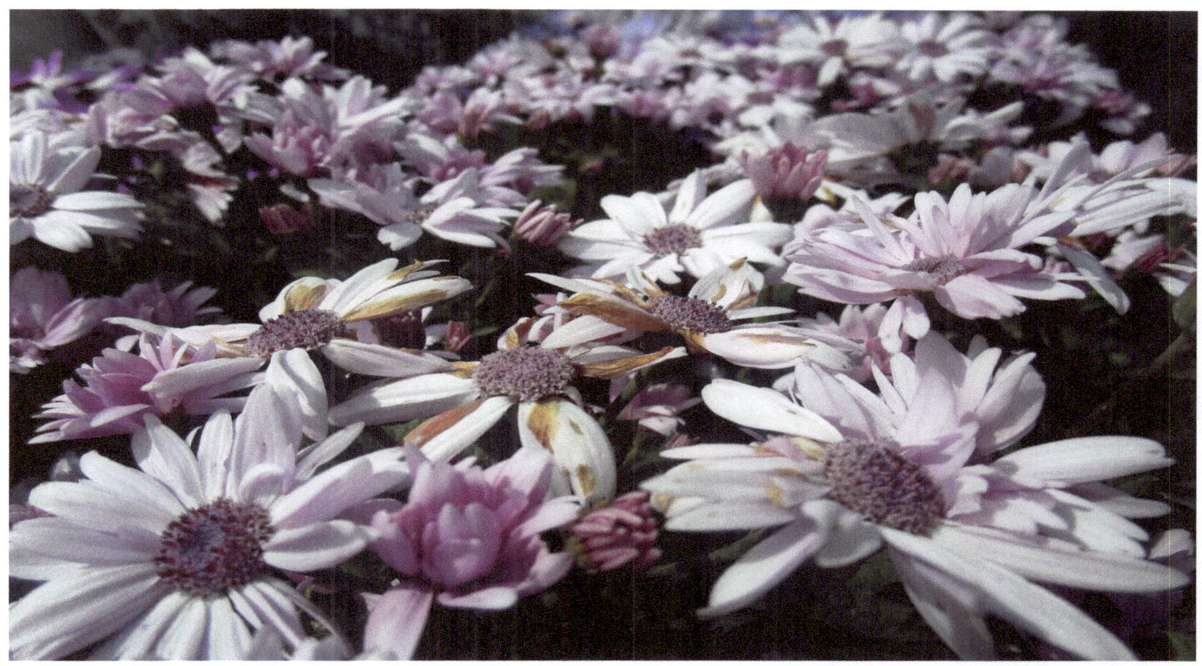

41. Shasta Daisy (Leucanthemum X superbum)
    Colour: White: Golden Yellow(Centre)
    First Bloom: June
    Amount of Sun Needed: Mild to Full
    Scent: Mild to Strong
    Petal Size: Medium

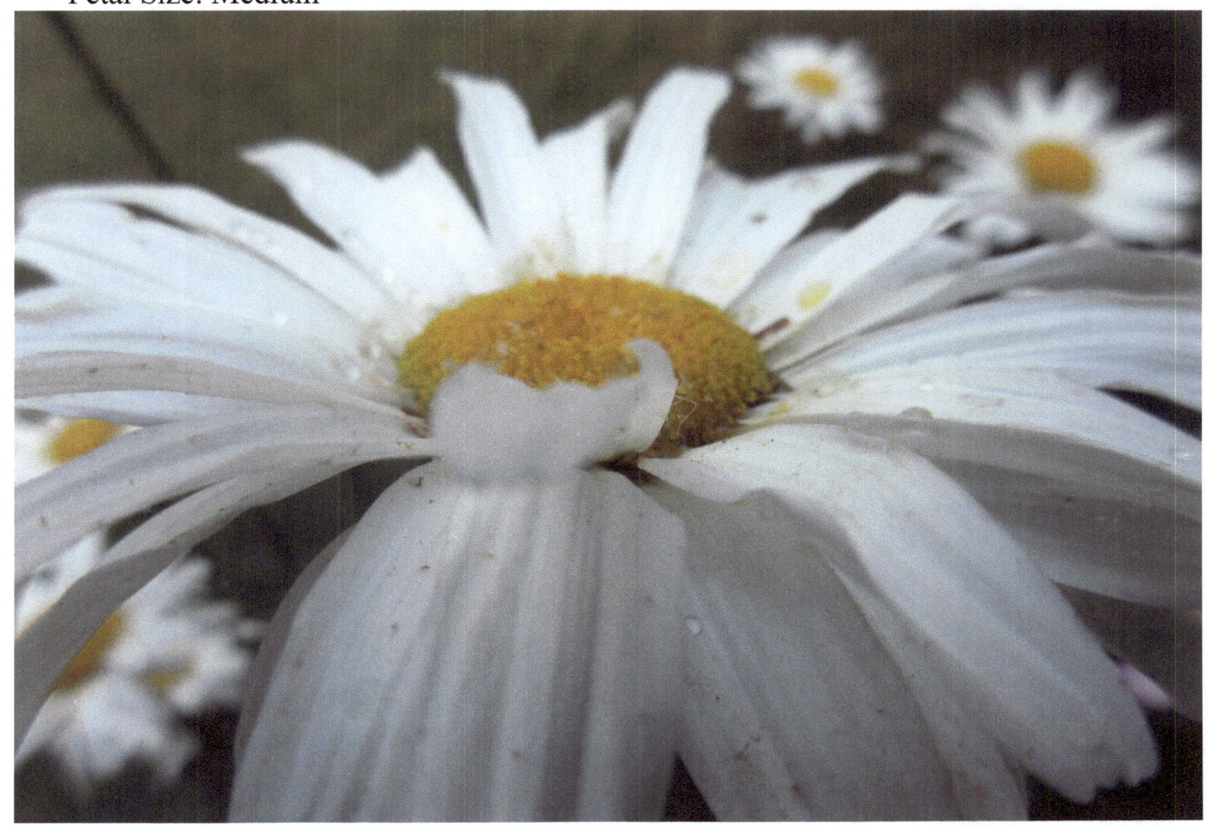

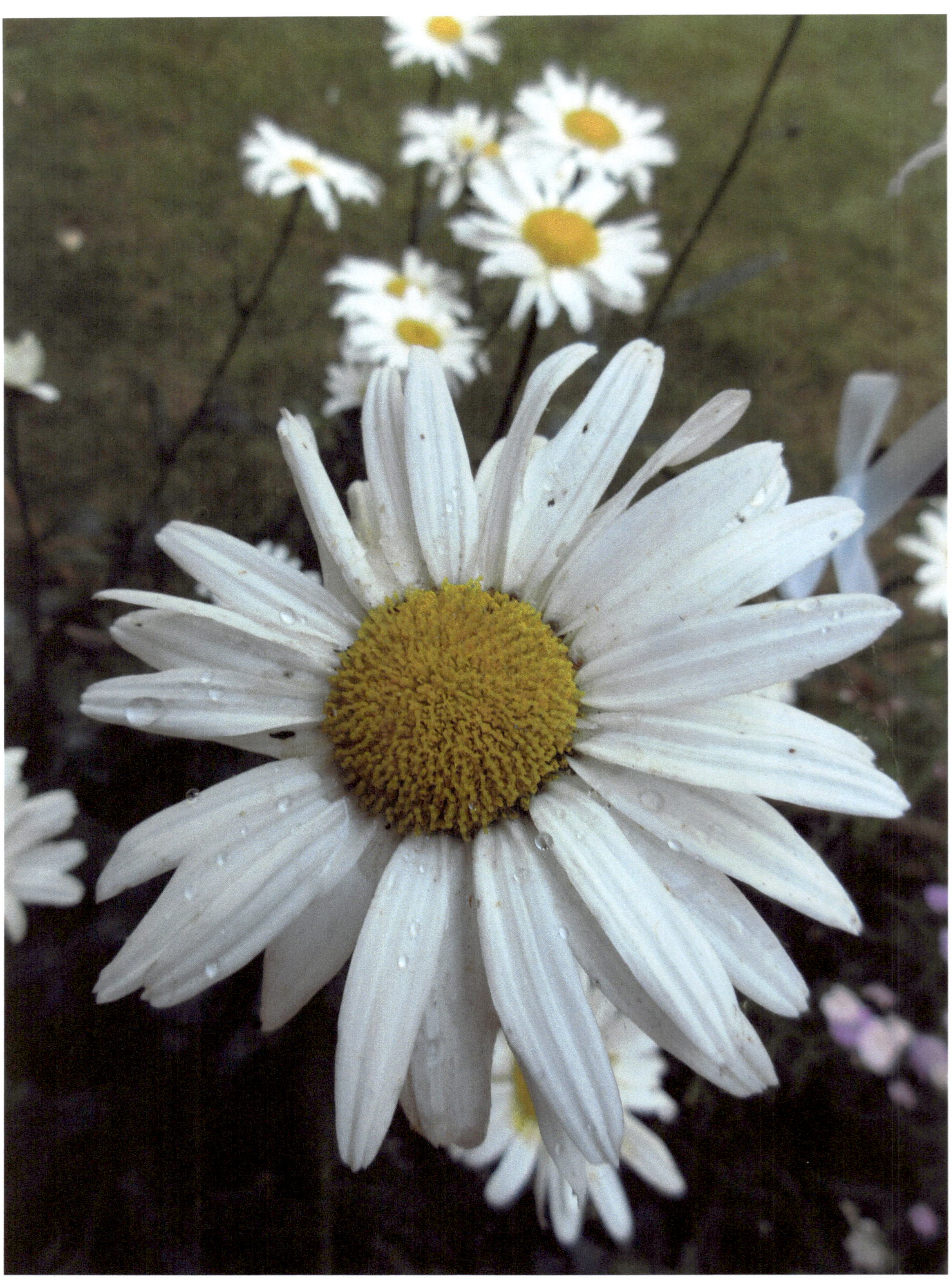

42. Tulip (Tulipa)
    Colour: Red; Yellow; Purple; Pink; White; Varied
    First Bloom: March
    Amount of Sun Needed: Moderate to Full
    Scent: None
    Petal Size: Medium to Fairly Large

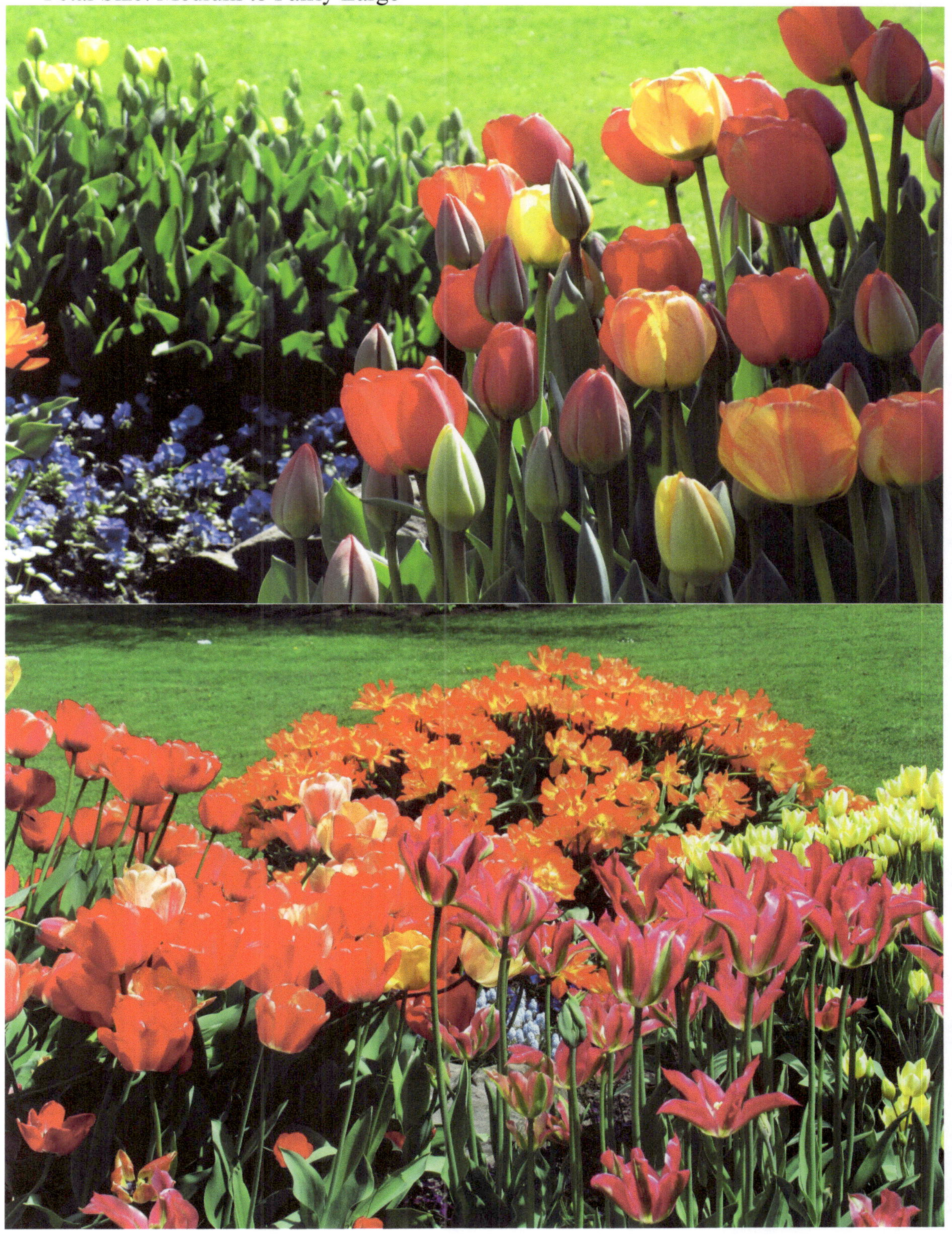

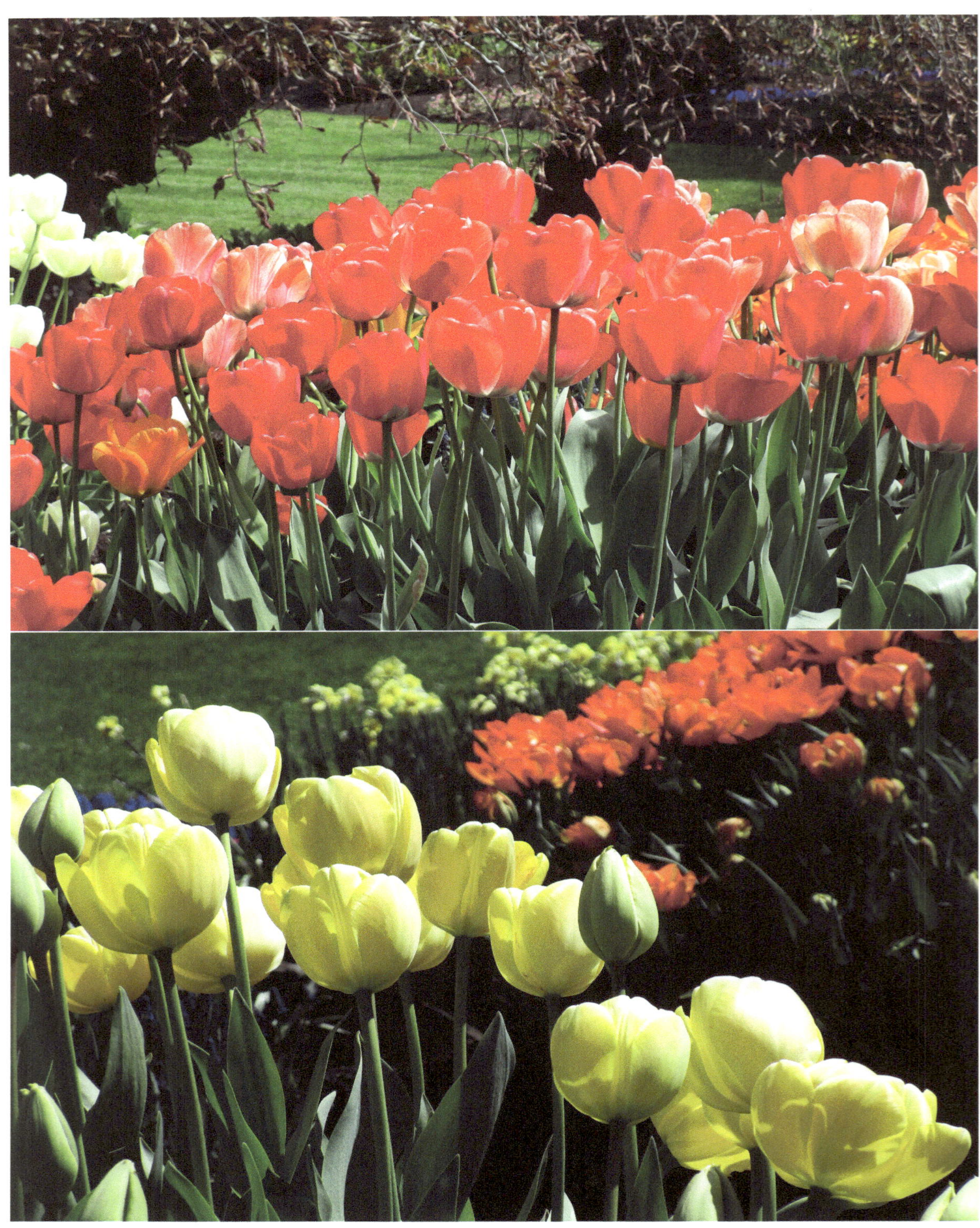

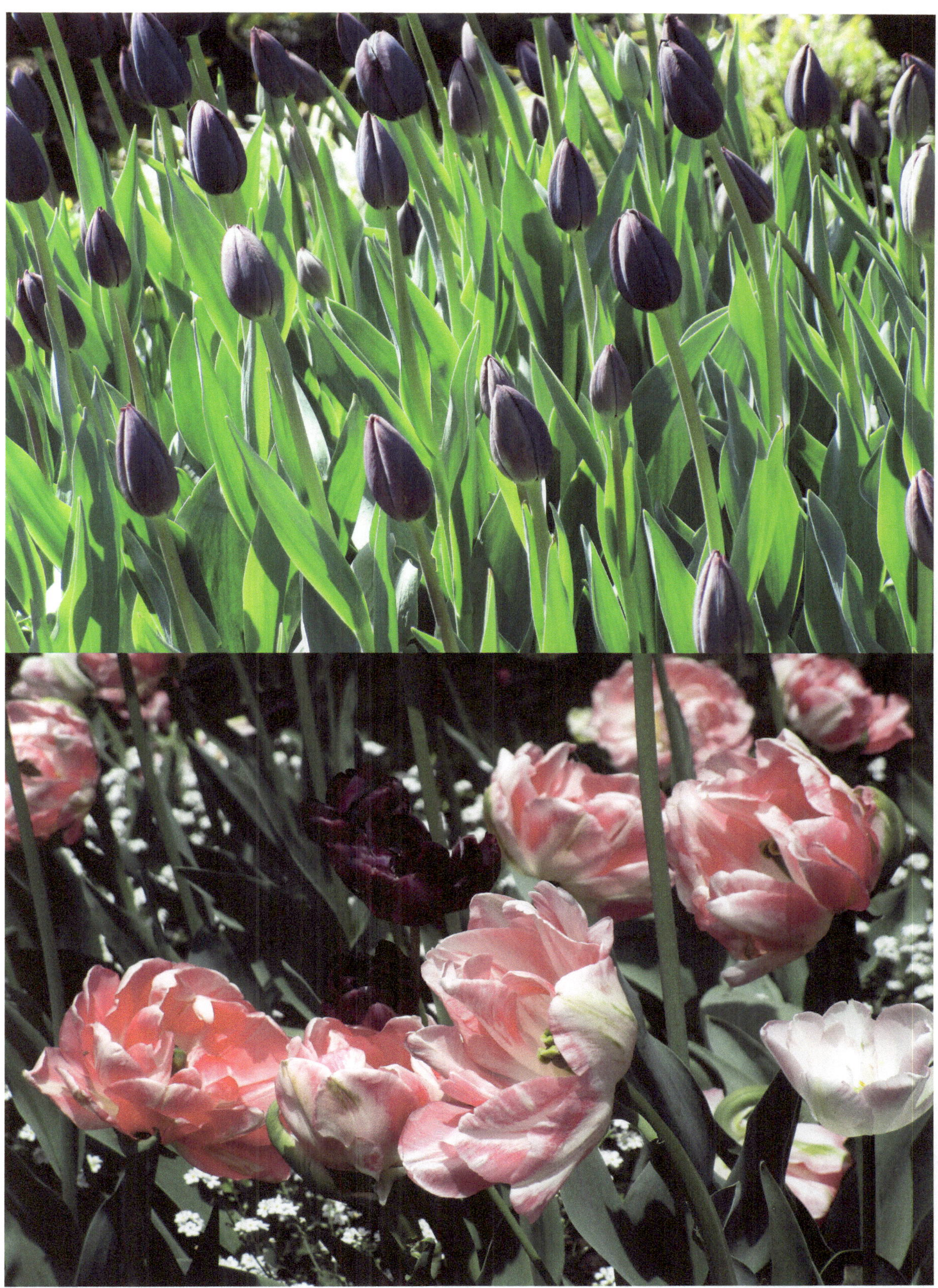

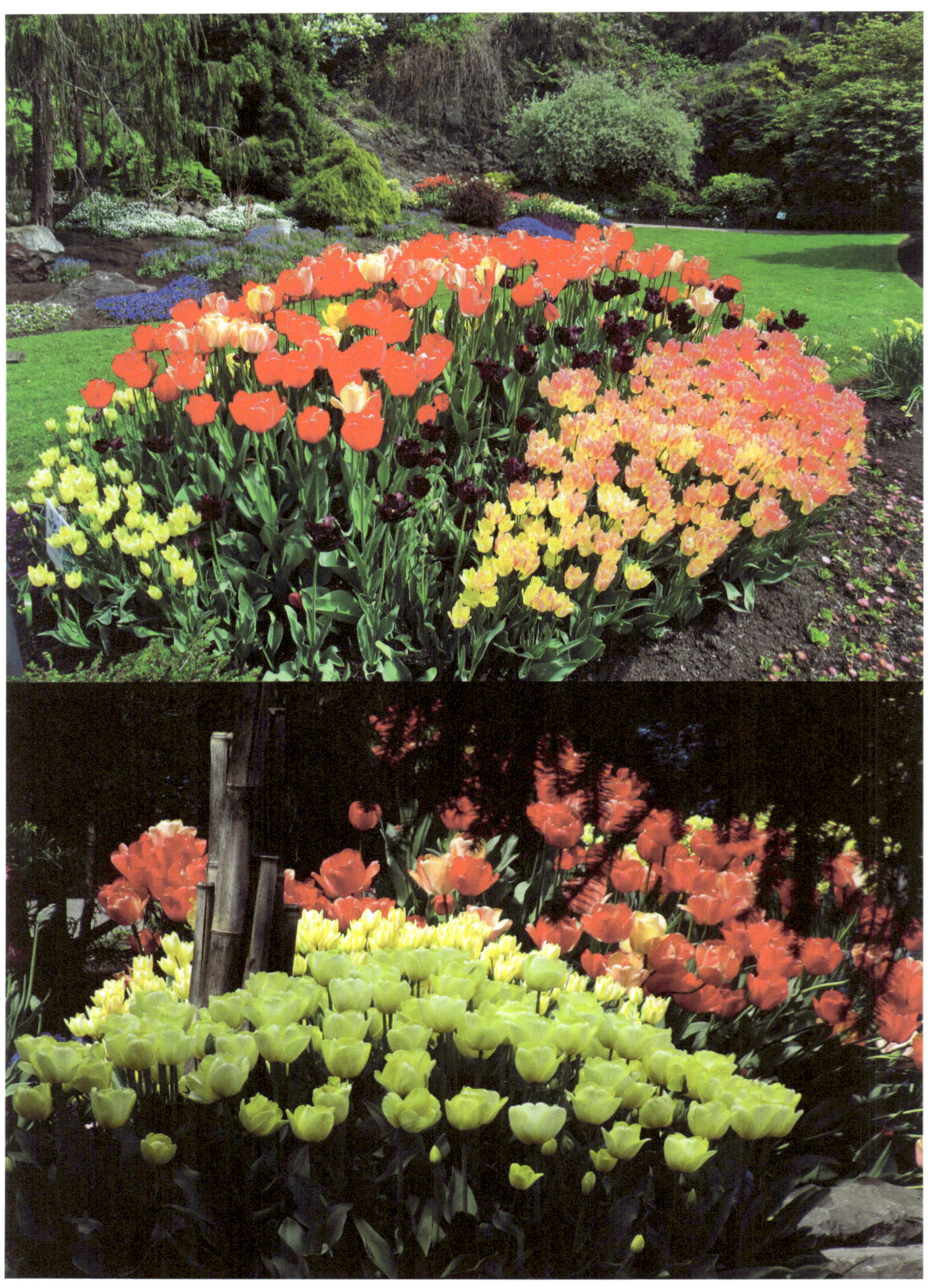

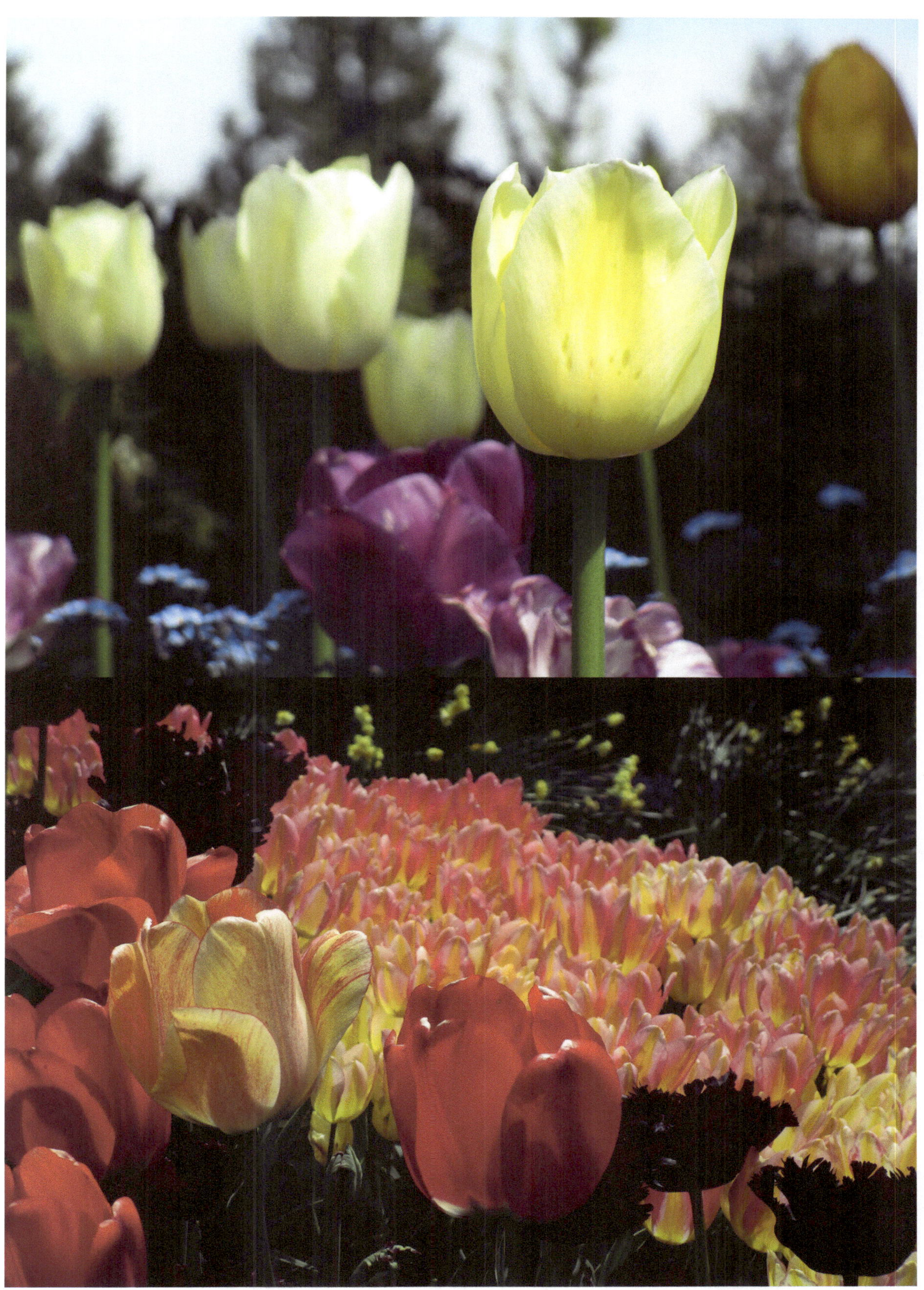

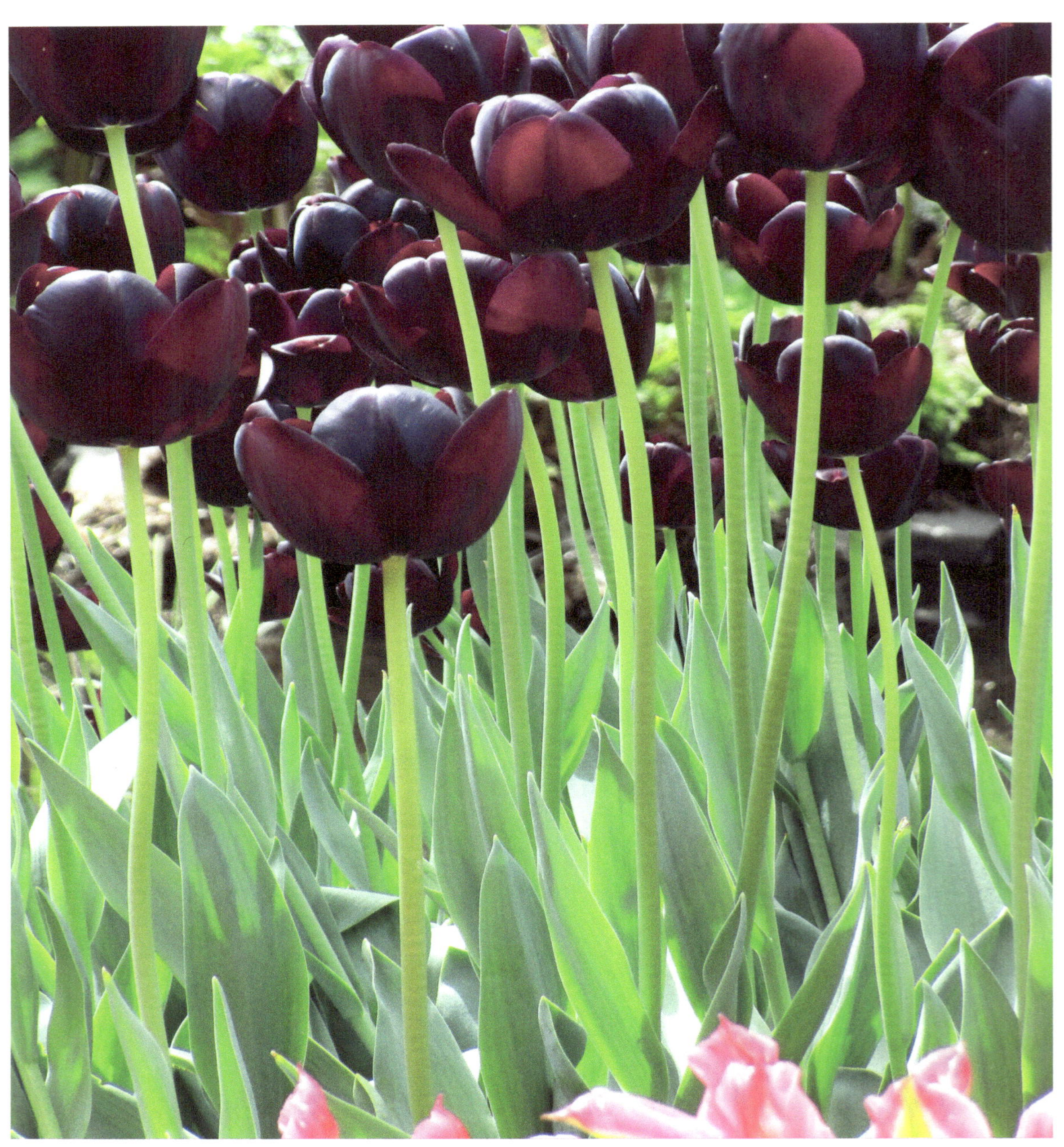

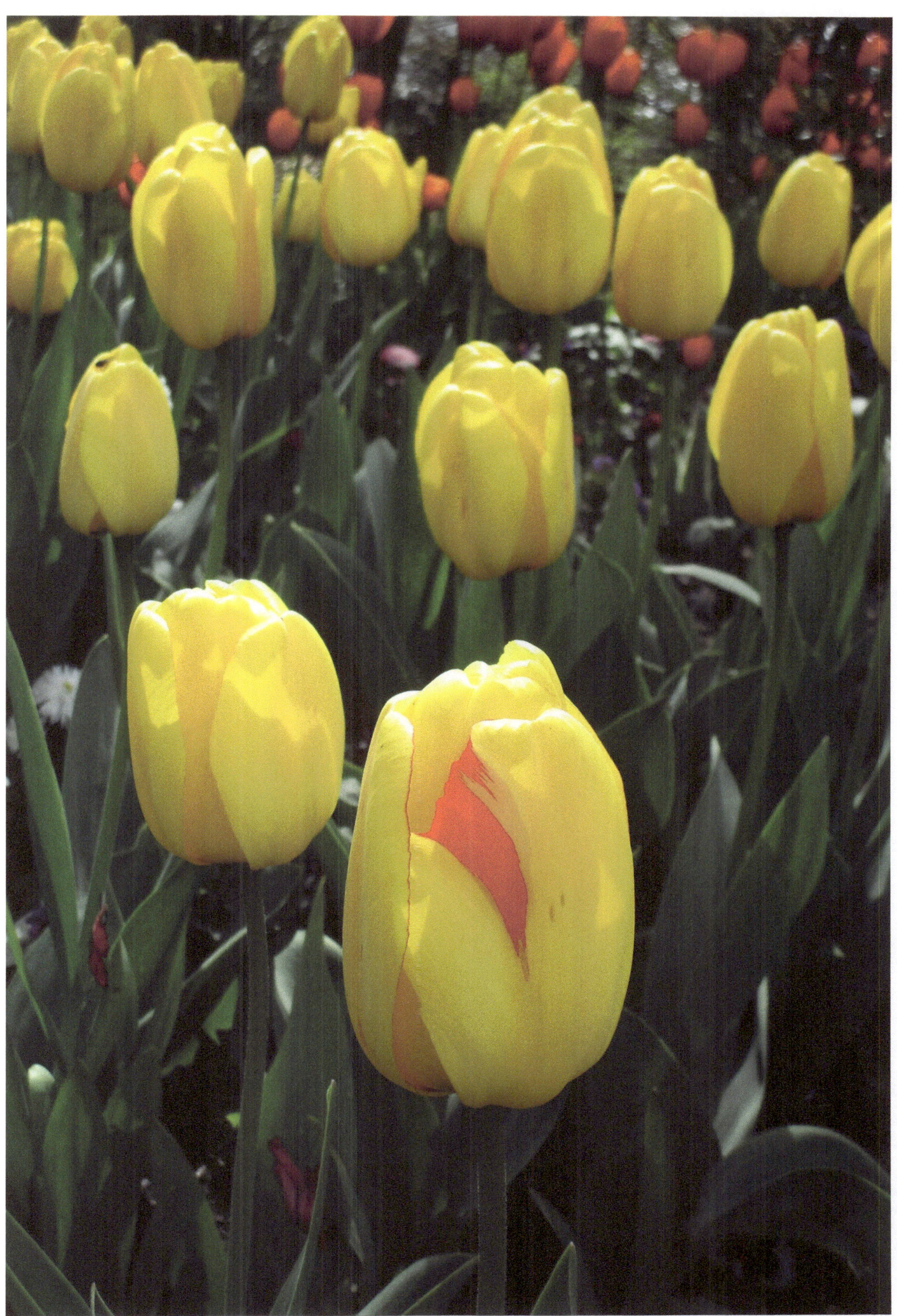

43. Verbena a.k.a. Vervain
    Colour: Purple; Violet
    First Bloom: August-September
    Amount of Sun Needed: Moderate to Full
    Scent: None
    Petal Size: Tiny

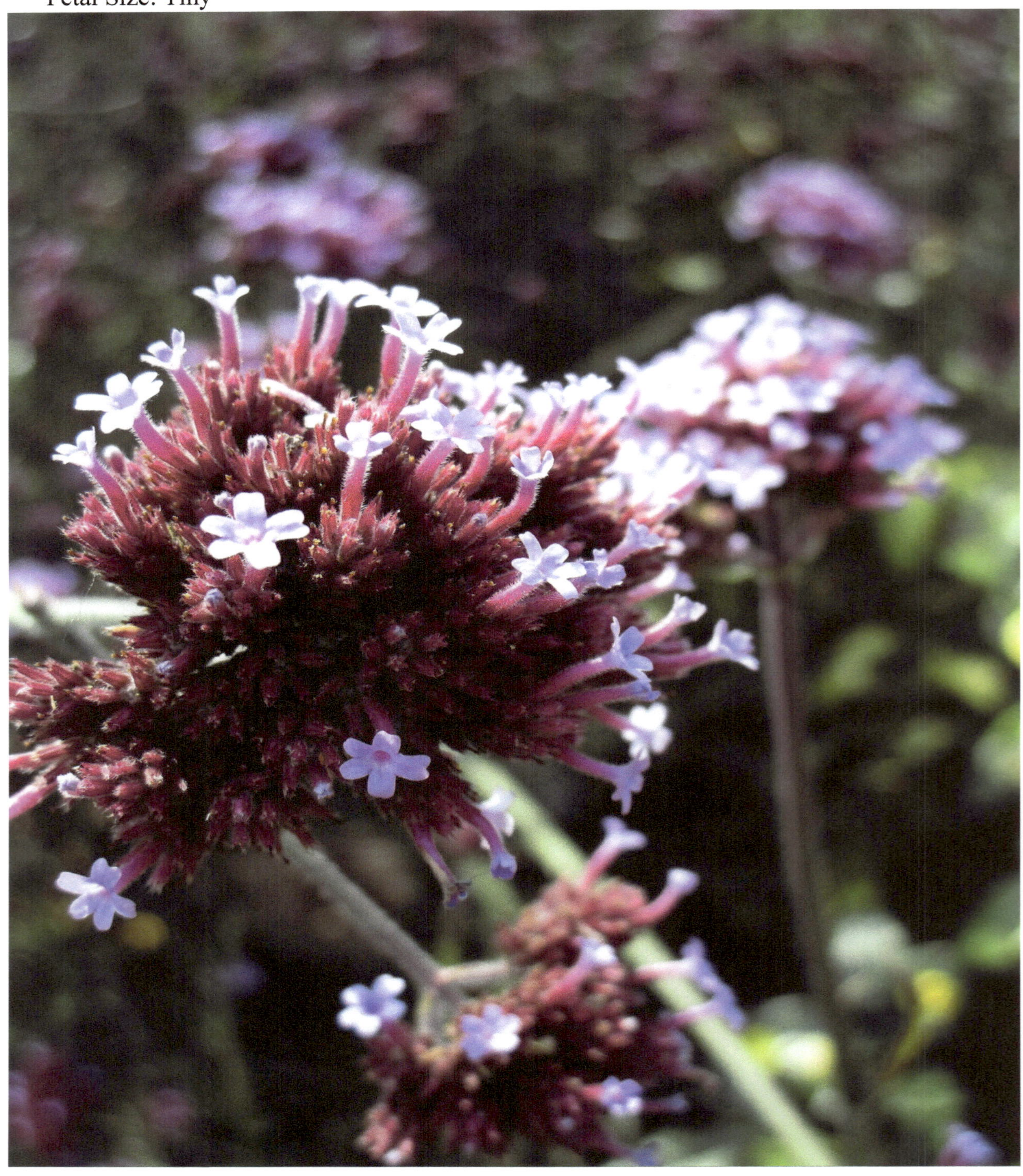

44. Virginia Spiderwort (Tradescantia virginiana)
    Colour: Bluish Purple, Yellow
    First Bloom: August
    Amount of Sun Needed: Mild to Moderate
    Scent: None
    Petal Size: Small to Fairly Medium

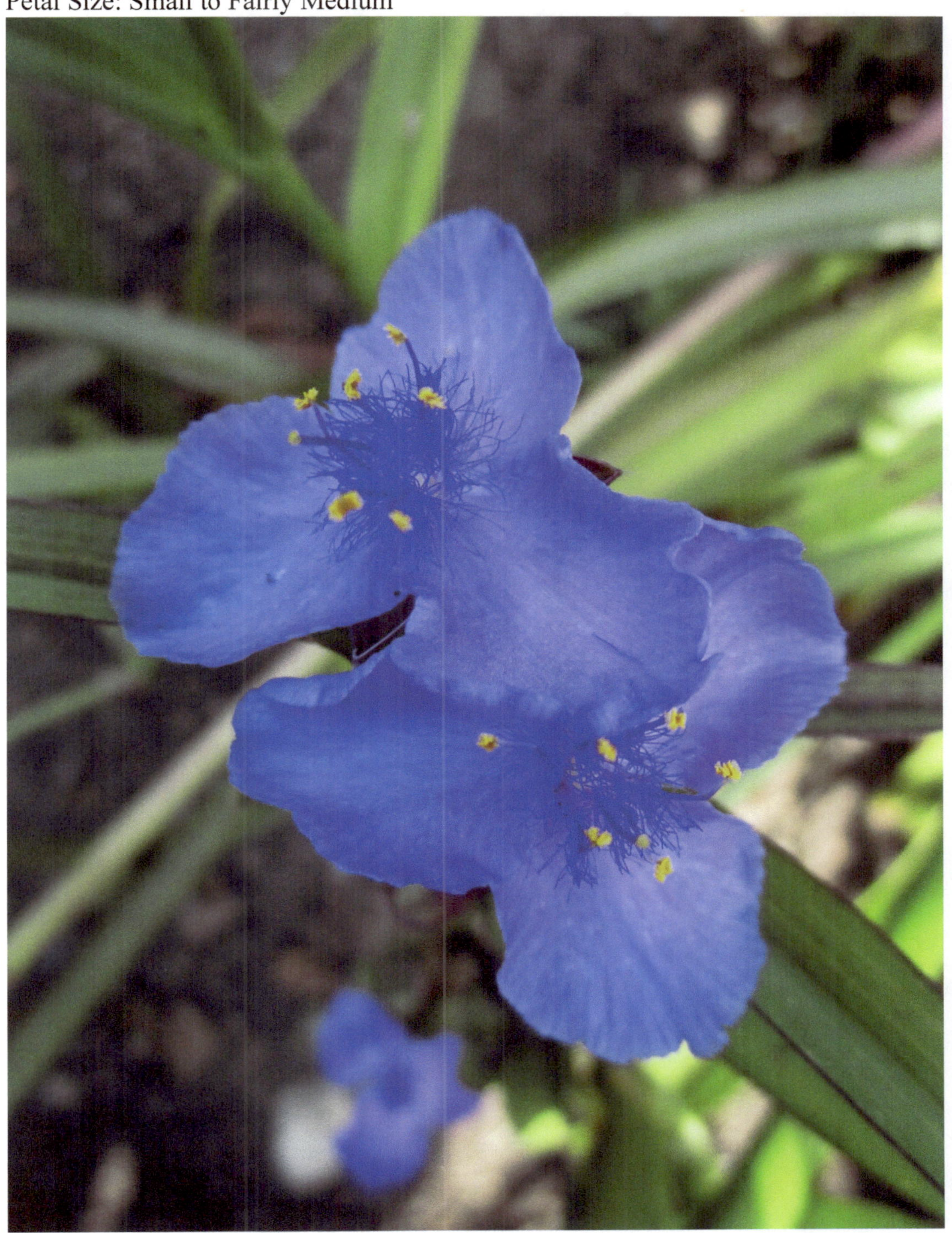

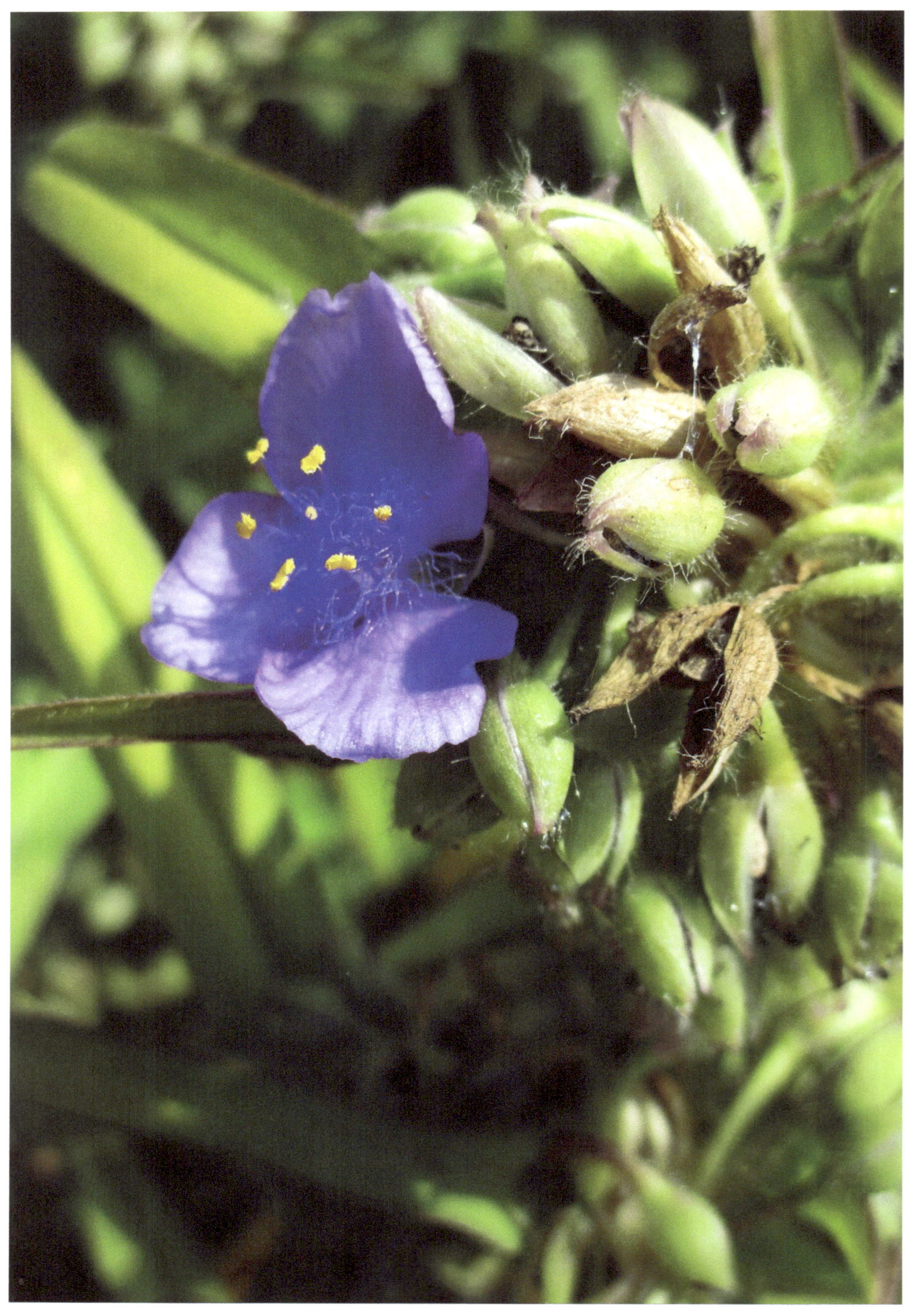

45. Weigela(Weigela)
   Colour: Red; Pink; White; Varied
   First Bloom: May
   Amount of Sun Needed: Mild
   Scent: None
   Petal Size: Small to Fairly Medium

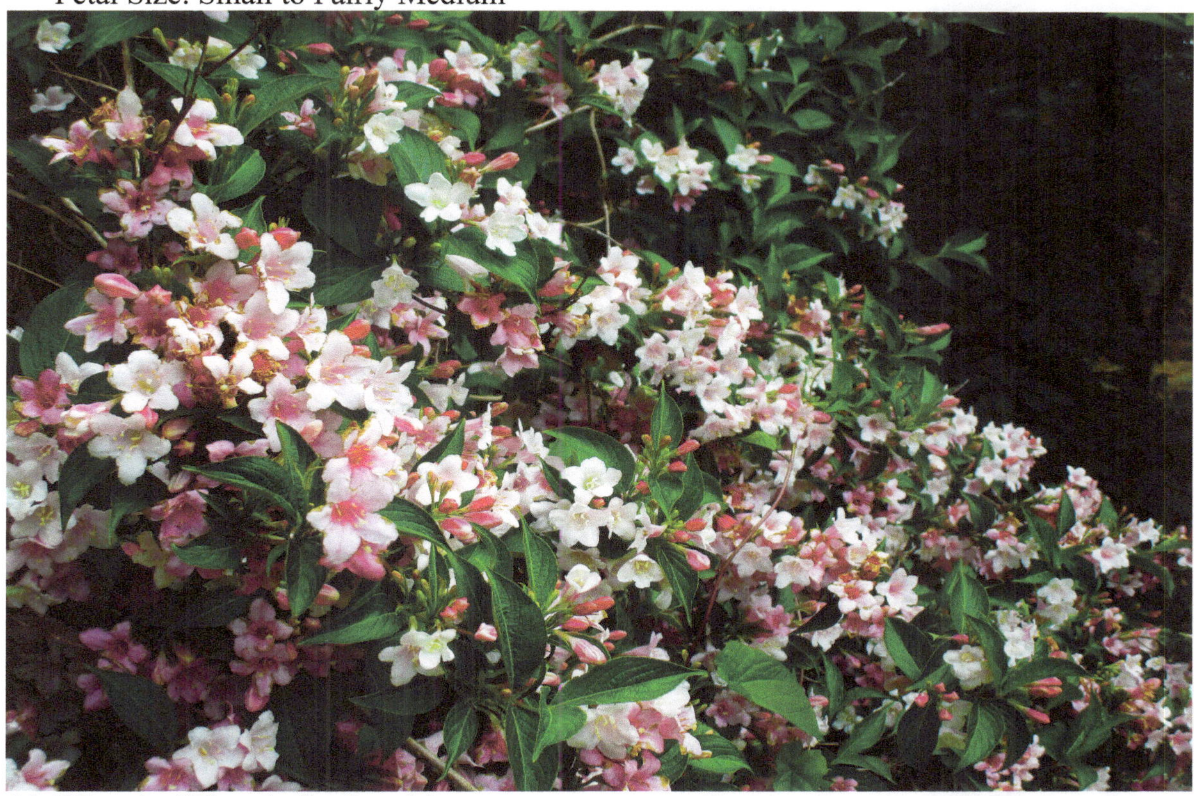

46. Wisteria (Wisteria floribunda)
   Colour: Purple; White; Yellow; Varied
   First Bloom: May
   Amount of Sun Needed: Moderate to Full
   Scent: None
   Petal Size: Small to Fairly Medium

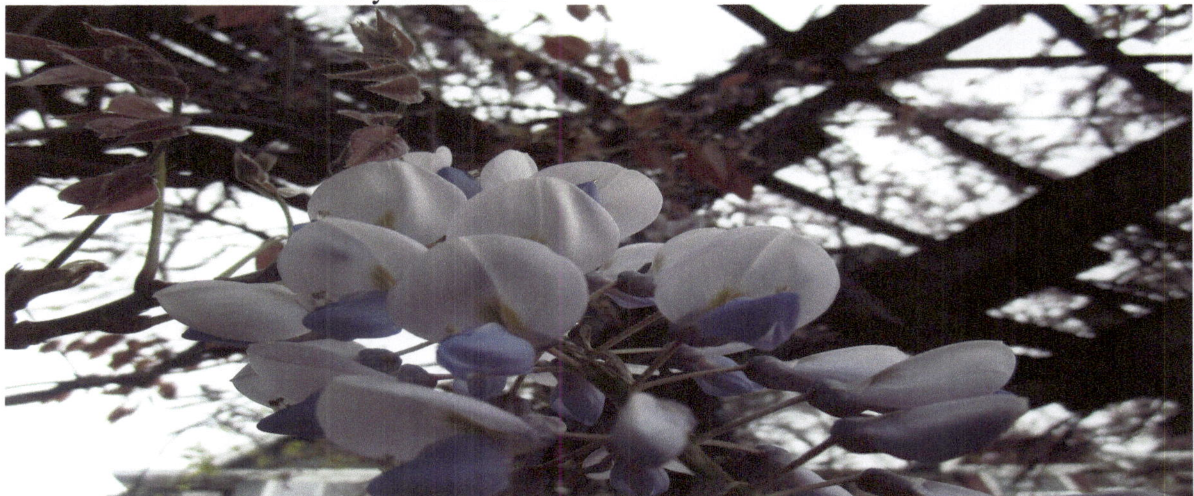

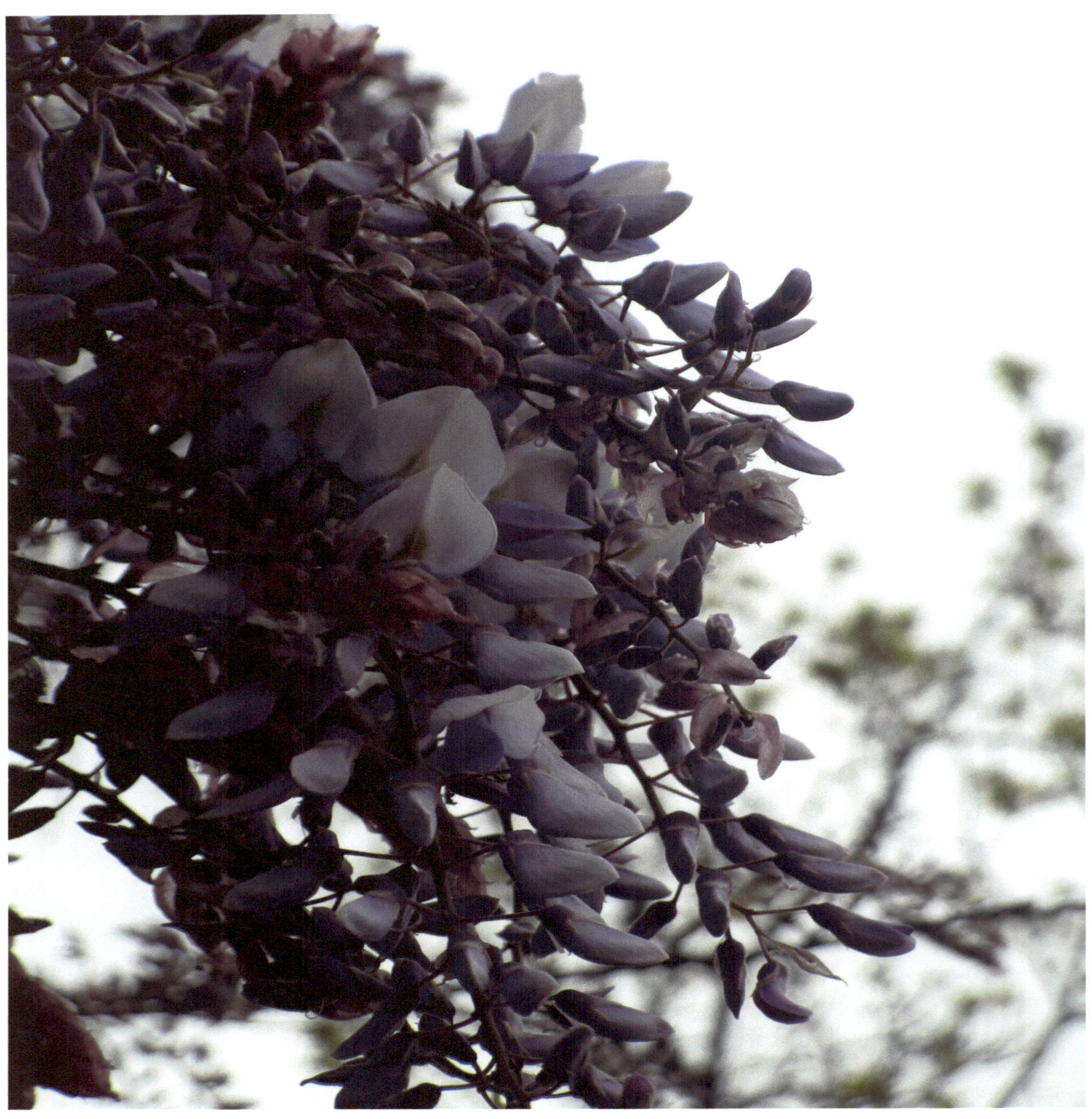

Japanese purple Wisteria in its early stage of bloom.

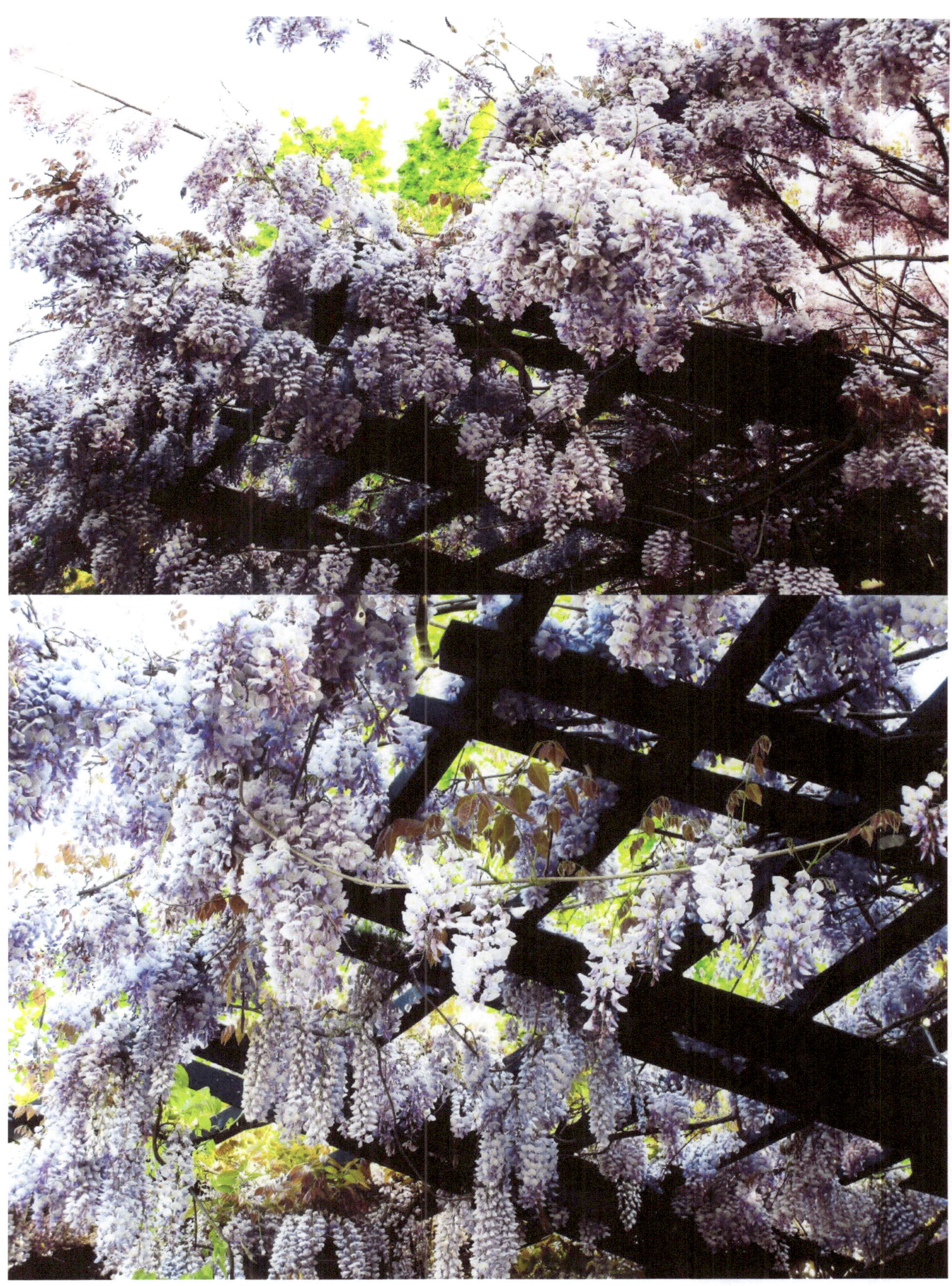

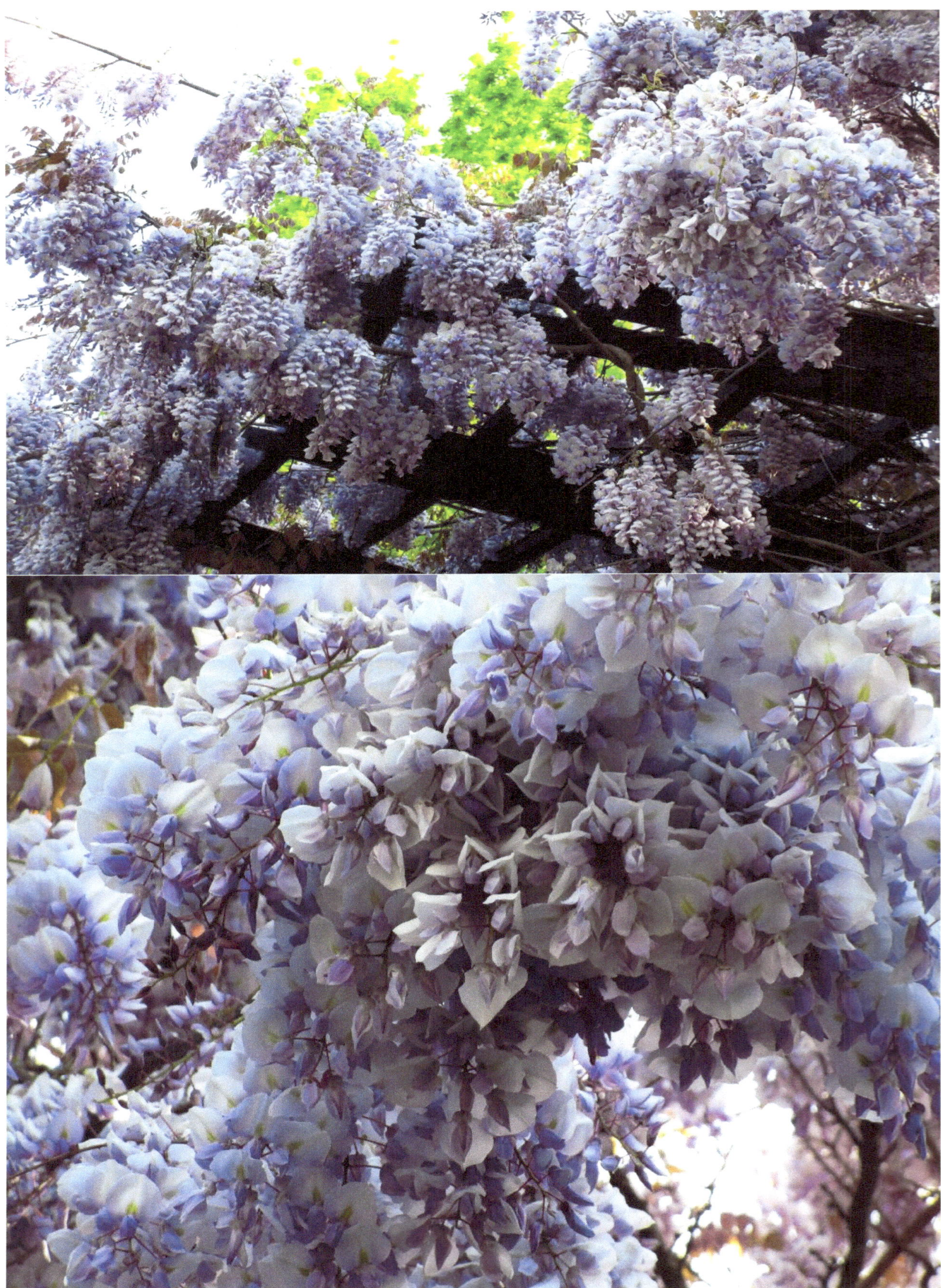

47. Yarrow (Achillea millefolium)
    Colour: White, Yellow
    First Bloom: June
    Amount of Sun Needed: Mild to Moderate
    Scent: None
    Petal Size: Considerably Small

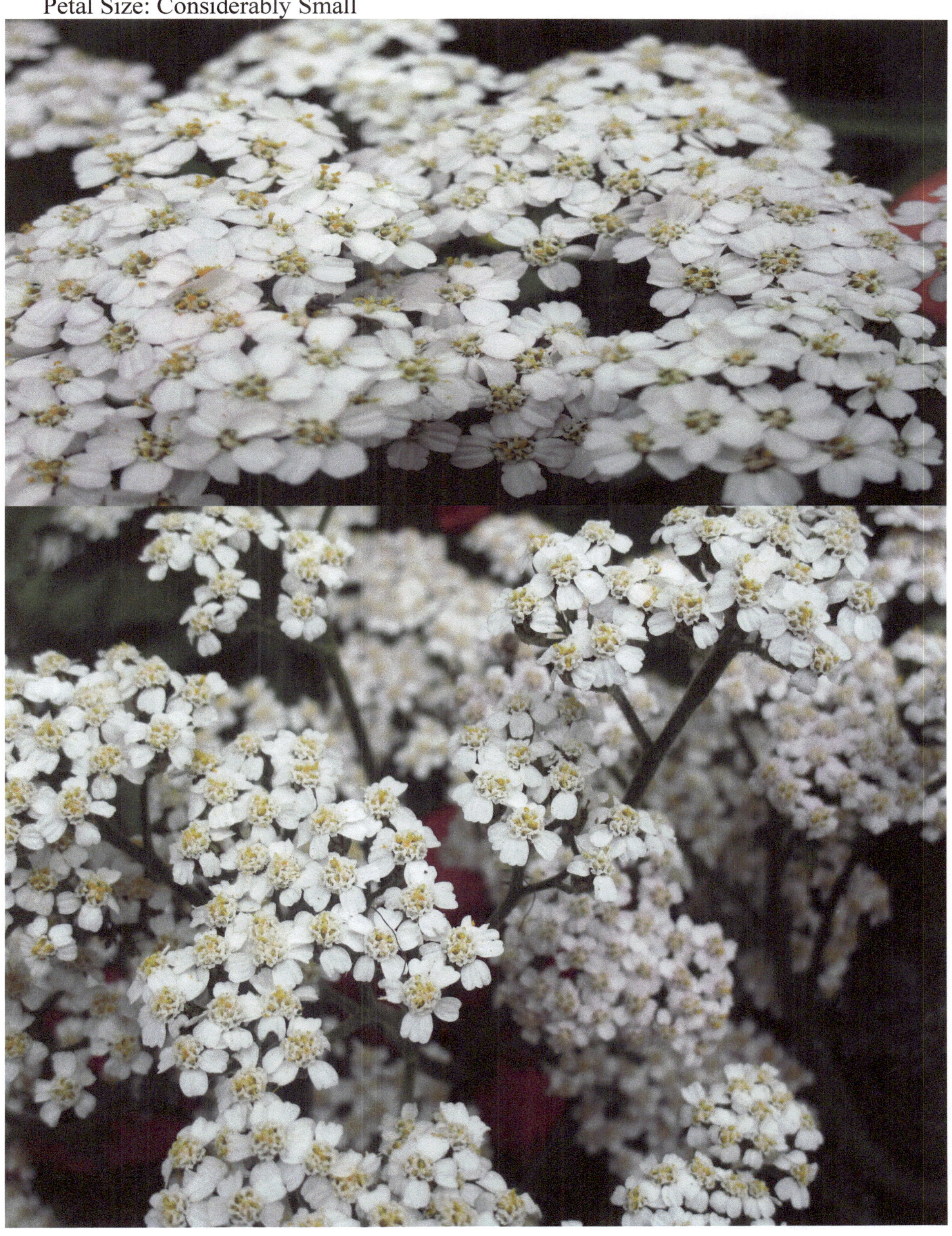

48. Yellow Coneflower (Echinacea)
    Colour: Yellow, Dark Brown(Centre)
    First Bloom: August
    Amount of Sun Needed: Moderate
    Scent: None
    Petal Size: Medium

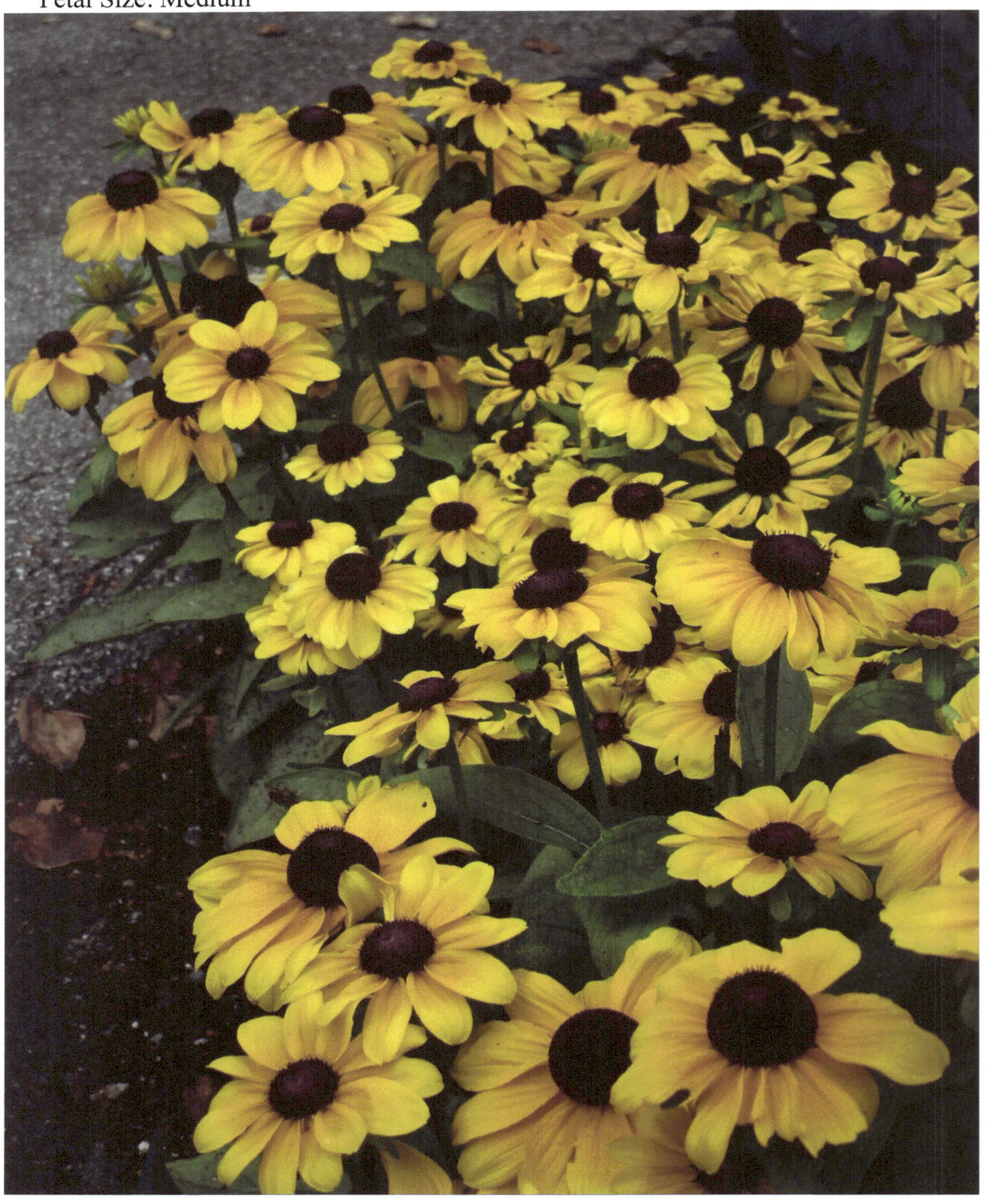